The Moneychangers of Wall Street

WHAT YOUR STOCKBROKER DOESN'T WANT YOU TO KNOW

H. Grant Perry

Pinehurst Capital, Inc.
PINEHURST, NORTH CAROLINA

H. Grant Perry/Pinehurst Capital, Inc.
100 Magnolia Road, 3rd Floor
Pinehurst, NC 28374
www.pinehurstcapital.net

Book layout ©2013 BookDesignTemplates.com

Ordering Information:
Quantity sales. Special discounts are available on quantity purchases by corporations, associations, and others. For details, contact the address above.

The Moneychangers of Wall Street/H. Grant Perry. —1st ed.
ISBN 978-1540567437

Contents

To my Dad, Herman. Thank you for all of the wonderful lessons that you taught me as a child, and for imparting upon me the value of a dollar. Love, Your Son, Grant a.k.a. Monkey

Preface

Perhaps the title of this book requires a little explanation.

Regardless of your religious persuasion, you have likely heard the story of Jesus chasing the moneychangers out of the temple in Jerusalem. It has always been a powerful part of the Gospel that appeals to me personally. He did it not once, but twice!

No one knows what Jesus looked like in the flesh, but this account in the Scriptures certainly dispels the notion that he was the weak and emaciated figure portrayed by some artists of the Middle Ages. In his first temple cleansing (John 2:13-17), Jesus bursts onto the scene like a superhero, brandishing a whip of ropes, overturning tables stacked with coins and chasing sheep and goats out of the temple.

What made the Messiah so upset? A little history here. Judea was ruled by the Romans, and the coin of the realm was Roman currency. The Jews, however, had their own coinage — the shekel — which was used for sacred worship at the temple. The moneychangers, or "money brokers" as some translations call them, turned a handsome profit by exchanging one currency for another. They did a booming business around Passover, when Jewish pilgrims flocked to the grand temple to offer up sacrifices.

The moneychangers weren't honest businessmen. They were hucksters and con-men who gouged these poor, unsuspecting travelers by overcharging them for the sheep, goats and doves they sold for sacrifices. Many of these people had traveled from distant lands and all they wanted to do was worship. What angered Jesus the most was they were being taken advantage of in a holy place.

Muscles bulging, jaw set, and fuming with righteous indignation, the Lord strode into the temple courtyard and taught those robe-wearing criminals a lesson in honest business practices. The scene described in the scriptures may seem at odds with the view of Jesus as a Prince of Peace who turns the other cheek at an insult. Keep in mind, however, he didn't hit anyone. The whip was not made for striking people. It was a "whip of ropes." He used it to shoo away smelly livestock from a place of worship. By overturning their money-laden tables, however, he let the moneychangers know in no uncertain terms that he disapproved of their little scam. Apparently, the lesson didn't stick. Three years later, he again came to the temple shortly before Passover and again turned their tables over and ran the moneychangers out of the temple.

Uncovering the Truth

One of the reasons I chose to write this book is because I have always had a passion for the truth. It irritates me to no end when people fiddle with the facts in order to sell you something. My father, Herman Perry, was a no-nonsense, farm-raised fellow who had no tolerance for lies or misinformation, and he must have passed the gene on to me. As a kid growing up in the rolling Sandhills of North Carolina, I would occasionally do something foolish that would displease my father. He was a strict disciplinarian — a facet of his personality I didn't appreciate then but do now. He asked straightforward questions and expected straightforward answers. For example: "Grant, did you _____?" You can fill in the blank with any number of things a young boy could get into on a farm. I learned early on that this was a tricky junction. I had a critical decision to make. Tell the truth — the naked and unvarnished truth — and things would usually go well. Lie to him, or try to hedge on my answer, and the consequences would be swift and unpleasant.

In the world of business and finance, there is no force quite as powerful or as compelling as full disclosure and telling things exactly the way they are. There is no substitute for honesty and candor.

I'm not trying to be a goodie-two-shoes when I say this, but my favorite book is The Bible. Not necessarily because of its literary style, but because of its powerful imagery and the life-lessons it conveys. When it comes to telling the truth, no book seems to stamp the principle of honesty and truth on our consciousness as indelibly as does the Good Book. Just a couple of my favorite verses are:

"Ye shall know the truth, and the truth shall make you free." (John 8:32)

"He that telleth lies shall not tarry in my sight." (Psalms 101:7)

What does exposing lies and telling the truth have to do with financial planning and retirement, you ask? Everything!

Misleading by Omission

A couple came into my office shortly after the 2008 stock market crash. The woman was almost in tears, and her husband wore a grave expression. They told me how hard they had worked and saved all of their lives. They had managed to put their two children through college and, by denying themselves many of the luxuries of life, had also managed to accumulate a nest egg of just under $600,000. She was a part-time nurse, and he owned a small landscaping business. Neither of them had a pension. They were counting on their retirement account to supplement their Social Security to provide them with a comfortable retirement. They were each 64 years old. They had planned to retire in 2009, but the financial crisis of 2008 changed all of that. They had lost nearly half of their life's savings, and to say they were unhappy with their financial advisor would be putting it mildly.

"Why didn't he tell us something like this could happen?" the woman asked.

This couple had been busy with work and life. They had left the management of their financial affairs to a "professional," and they had felt sure they were in good hands. When the bottom started to drop out of the market, they asked their broker whether they should cut their losses and convert their holdings to cash.

"He told us just to hang in there," said the woman. "He said the market has ups and downs and this was just one of the downs."

Did the stockbroker tell this couple the truth? Yes, in a way. The stock market does ebb and flow. There are ups and downs. And historically, after a stock market reversal, stock prices do recover, *eventually*. The problem here was this couple did not have *eventually* to wait. Whether it was intentional or not, this financial advisor failed this couple by (a) not taking their ages into account and (b) by failing to disclose all of the facts.

In our interview, the husband acknowledged that he had not taken enough responsibility for the couple's finances. "We didn't ask enough questions," he said. He was right about that. Does that let this financial advisor off the hook? No. The couple probably didn't know the right questions to ask. A competent financial advisor who had their best interests at heart would have been more sensitive to their financial goals in life and would have informed them of the potential downside of having their entire life's savings at risk in the market. When it comes to matters of finance, the omission of pertinent and vital information can be just as damaging as an outright lie.

Lying Statistics

Mark Twain said, "There are lies, damned lies, and statistics." Take averages, for example. Averages can be useful to us in many ways. By knowing the average number of motorists who use a section of highway, road planners can decide whether they should add more lanes. A nutritionist needs to know the average number of calories an individual consumes before he or she can help them lose weight.

People who want to mislead you will sometimes play naughty tricks with the numbers and present it as logic.

A man may boast, "My wife and I ride our bicycles an average of 10 miles every day." Immediately, your mind conjures up an image of two health-conscious people getting up perhaps every morning to pedal 10 miles together down a country lane. The truth is, she is the one who gets up at dawn for a 20-mile bike ride while he hits the snooze button and sleeps in. The guy didn't lie, though, did he? He just tricked you with numbers.

Our home office is located in the charming Village of Pinehurst, North Carolina, population 15,255 (unless, that is, a professional golf tournament is going on). You could put the average household income of Pinehurst at approximately $68,500, and you would be right. But what would happen to that figure if Warren Buffett and Bill and Melinda Gates moved into town? What would that do to the average income statistics of our little town? It would make the average income statistic misleading and meaningless.

As you continue reading, you will encounter several examples of myths, miscalculations, and mathematical tricks that Wall Street likes to play. You will learn how to separate investing truth from investing fiction. We will ferret out hidden fees and uncloak unnecessary taxes and investing costs that rob millions of America's investors of prosperity they need in their retirement.

As my father used to say, "Truth has its own license to speak." So I really can't apologize for pulling back the curtain and exposing a few of Wall Street's most egregious sleight-of-hand tricks. But this book is not just about exposing myths and uncovering hidden fees. We will also discuss straightforward and transparent strategies that many modern investors are beginning to embrace, but that Wall Street would prefer you didn't know about. So, please keep an open mind when you read about them. Some of them may lead you in a fresh and new direction of thinking. Sometimes the most effective way to accomplish a financial goal is the simplest. And, more often than not, the quickest route from point A to point B is a simple straight line.

CHAPTER 1

Emotions and Peace of Mind

"Even the intelligent investor is likely to need considerable willpower to keep from following the crowd."
—BENJAMIN GRAHAM

While doing some research the other day on the internet, one of those pesky little pop-up ads caught my eye. You know — the ones that appear on the right side of the screen. I usually ignore them, but this one got my attention: *"New Computer App Replacing Human Financial Advisors."*

Since I am a human financial advisor, I was curious as to just what sort of new device or gizmo the world of technology had come up with to replace me. As I read on I learned the app was something called "FutureAdvisor."

The next line read, "FutureAdvisor Brings Mint-Style Advice to Investors." I knew about Mint©. It is a handy little personal accounting program that organizes all your accounts into one place and identifies your spending habits at a glance. But FutureAdvisor? What was that all about? For some reason, an image flashed through my mind of that robot on the old TV show, "Lost in

Space," pointing his bulky arm at me, saying in that robot voice, "Greetings from the future, Grant Perry. You are being replaced. Clean out your desk and don't let the door hit you on the way out."

The ad went on to say that FutureAdvisor was free. Really? Nothing is free, I thought to myself. I scrolled down until I found the revealing paragraph in finer print. The app was free, but you had to pay $195 for a "Platinum" level membership.

Here's the way it works: You plug in your account information — IRAs, 401(k)s, investment accounts, etc. — then answer a series of questions, such as your current age, desired retirement age, risk tolerance, retirement goals, etc. FutureAdvisor then gives you recommendations each month as to how to invest your money — **"with emphasis on mutual funds"** the ad said.

I couldn't help but smile at that last part. Mutual funds are a mystery to most investors. They know what mutual funds are, but understand little about how they work. Mutual funds are a labyrinth of complexity and there are as many types of mutual funds as there are models of cars on the road. According to U.S. News and World Report©, at the end of 2012 there were 7,238 mutual funds in operation and "one of the investing industry's most uncomfortable truths is that a huge number of them fail." [1]

Back to my electronic replacement. As famous radio personality Paul Harvey used to say, "the rest of the story" appeared at the bottom of the ad in small print. Apparently this new "automated financial advisor" was backed by a California venture-capital firm. If you followed the recommendations made by the electronic financial advisor, somewhere down the line, a living, breathing human would execute the trade *and make a commission on the deal.* (I knew there had to be a human in there somewhere).

Way at the bottom of the ad in fine print was this disclaimer:

---

[1] Rob Silverblatt. U.S. News: Money. June 10, 2013. "Are There Too Many Mutual Funds?" http://money.usnews.com/money/personal-finance/mutual-funds/articles/2013/06/10/are-there-too-many-mutual-funds. Accessed Sept. 23, 2016.

"The content on this site is for informational and educational purposes only and should not be construed as professional financial advice. Should you need such advice, consult a licensed financial or tax advisor. References to products, offers, and rates from third party sites often change."

The Emotions of Investing

Robotics has revolutionized the manufacturing industry — why not investing? I could see why some might find the idea of automated investing attractive. It would lift from them all the responsibility of making decisions. It would also remove emotions from the process of managing money. Dealing with money involves our feelings. All of our hopes, our fears, and our plans for the future are intertwined with how we feel about — and how we deal with — money. How we budget it, how we spend it, and how we save it for retirement — all of these elements are tangled with deep emotions.

While emotions can be helpful in many elements of life, they can also prevent us from making the most rational decisions about how to best use our money to make our lives better. Unless you have an expert to help you, it can be scary and overwhelming. Fear and anxiety can override common sense.

A good financial advisor understands that and aims to help clients feel less fear and more confidence in their choices. One vivid example is that of an 80-year-old widow who became a client of ours after her husband had passed away. During the course of her marriage, she had taken care of the house, her husband, the children, and practically everything else. But she never involved herself with finances. She was never consulted when decisions regarding money came up. She entrusted all that business to her capable husband. She had a checkbook, but she had never learned how to balance it. Her husband's death was traumatic for her on several levels, not the least of which were her worries about how to manage her personal finances. It wasn't that she lacked money. In fact, her husband had left her a sizable portfolio of stocks and other investments. But she knew practically nothing about them.

When she turned to us for help, we knew this would be a case of patiently working with her from square one — from how to pay bills and balance her checkbook all the way to managing her personal wealth. She was an intelligent woman. But she found making rational financial decisions difficult. Why? Because her emotions were involved. She wanted someone to make her money decisions for her. We could have done that, but it would not have served her best interests. She needed to be self-reliant. She needed someone to de-mystify the world of finance and teach her what she needed to know. As we worked with her, the grief she felt over losing her husband gradually subsided. Her confidence about making financial decisions grew as her base of knowledge increased. Within two years, she was comfortable enough to make rational financial decisions for the first time in her life.

This story illustrates well why it is imperative that both spouses attend meetings with their financial advisor. Both spouses should be involved in the major decisions in life, especially when it comes to the family finances. It usually only takes one discussion for couples to see how vital this is.

Planning Ahead Financially

Can you imagine setting out on a journey without a destination in mind? I can't either. To quote Yogi Berra, the master of malapropisms, "If you don't know where you're going, you may not get there."

In a study released in December of 2014, the American College of Financial Services® provided the results of a poll of more than 1,000 people between the ages of 60 and 75 who had at least $100,000 in household assets. They answered questions on a variety of topics, from life expectancy to Social Security, IRAs, life insurance and other investments. The results showed that only two in 10 — only 20 percent — received a passing grade.

Among the American College of Financial Services® other findings:

- Only 1 in 4 has a written financial plan.
- A significant number of people have never calculated how much they must accumulate to have a secure retirement.
- Less than 1/3 (31 percent) realize that $2,800, adjusted annually for inflation, is the most they can afford to withdraw per year from a $100,000 retirement in order for it to last 30 years.
- More than half underestimate the life expectancy of a 65-year-old person and do not realize how long their assets must last.
- Only 54 percent know that Social Security benefits increase every year one delays claiming them — up to age 70. Roughly the same number of respondents knew to defer claiming benefits until age 70 if they expected to live to age 90 or older. [2]

We Are Living Longer

The good news is we are living longer. The bad news, at least from a financial planning point of view, is we are living longer. Don't get me wrong. I want to live as long as I can, and I am sure you do, too. But studies reveal that the biggest fear people have is outliving their resources. Running out of money in our old age translates into losing our independence. Who wants to run out of

---

[2] The American College of Financial Services: Bryn Maur, PA. Dec. 3, 2014. "Crash Course Needed: Four out of Five Americans Fail When Quizzed on How to Make Their Nest Eggs Last."

money in old age and end up becoming a burden on his or her loved ones? No one.

In October 2014, the Society of Actuaries© (SOA) released a study that shows the life expectancy for 65-year-old men is an average of 86.6 years. The same study shows the average life expectancy for women to be 88.8 years. (These figures represent at least a two-year increase in life expectancy compared to the Social Security Administration's estimates from the year 2000.) Keep in mind, those numbers are merely averages. The way longevity statistics are calculated, the longer you live, the longer you will live. In other words, if you make it to 75, you have a better chance of living to age 90 and beyond. According to the SOA, one out of every four 65-year-olds will live to the age of 90, and one in 10 will make it to 95. As we get deeper into the 21st century, the average life expectancy is expected to continue to rise. Are you prepared, financially, to live that long?

The Society of Actuaries© studies also show a majority of retirees underestimate their expected lifespan — a miscalculation that can have a significant impact on their long-term financial situation. The studies show that genetics and family medical history can have as much as a 50 percent impact on expected lifespan, but that lifestyle and diet also play a critical role. (The Society's 2011 report also indicated that improved longevity of college graduates is roughly double that of the population as a whole.)

As the American population ages, there is an almost infinite explosion of retirement planning choices and options. Unless you are working with a professional, independent fiduciary advisor, it can be overwhelming — almost paralyzing — to make the right choices for you and your family.

Do you have the correct retirement plan in place? Does that plan enrich your broker with high, perhaps hidden fees, or does it enrich you and enhance your life?

Are you exposed to unnecessary risks in your investments?

Do you know how much you are being charged?

Are you providing the best financial security possible for yourself, your spouse, and your children? [3]

Work With a Fiduciary

Fiduciary is a word we don't use in everyday conversation. It comes from the Latin word for **truth** or **trust**. As an investor, you must understand the difference between two competing standards — *fiduciary* and *suitability.*

Fiduciary Standard

The Investment Advisers Act of 1940 mandates that advisors so designated must place the interests of the client ahead of their own. Their conduct in this regard is regulated by the Securities and Exchange Commission (SEC). Fiduciaries are not captive agents working for one company; they are independent. This frees them to assist clients in achieving their financial objectives. This elevates them to the position of problem solvers, not product salespeople.

Suitability Standard

This ethics standard requires that the advisor refrain from making recommendations that are not suitable for a client. It ensures, for example, that transaction costs will not be excessive. The suitability standard would prevent an advisor from misusing his or her relationship with a client by churning (excessive trading) just to earn extra commissions. Those are good things, but

---

[3] Society of Actuaries (as seen on PR Newswire). Oct. 27, 2014. "Society of Actuaries Releases New Mortality Tables and an Updated Mortality Improvement Scale to Improve Accuracy of Private Pension Plan Estimates." http://www.prnewswire.com/news-releases/society-of-actuaries-releases-new-mortality-tables-and-an-updated-mortality-improvement-scale-to-improve-accuracy-of-private-pension-plan-estimates-245512447.html. Accessed Sept. 22, 2016.

the suitability standard allows its adherents to work for a single company and sell only its products.

Stockbrokers and broker-dealers work under the banner of the suitability standard. Their recommendations merely have to be suitable; but in other respects to the products they are recommending, they are ethically and legally able to put their own interests ahead of the investor. A stockbroker is, in essence, a salesperson whose job is to sell the products approved by his or her broker-dealer. An independent fiduciary, on the other hand, is not tethered by company loyalty and can recommend unlimited choices.

The difference may be illustrated this way: If you walk into a Ford® dealership, you are probably under no delusion that the salesperson will do a thorough analysis of all the autos on the market, compare prices and services, arrange for you to test-drive the top five makes and models that meet your criteria, and assist you in making

> "If you only have a hammer, you tend to see every problem as a nail."
> ~ABRAHAM LASLOW

a rational and educated decision on which one to buy. No. You are in a Ford® dealership. The salesperson will sell you a Ford®. In fact, the salesperson will be fired if he or she *doesn't* attempt to sell you a Ford®. They are not working with you in a fiduciary capacity. Neither are stockbrokers. They may offer you a variety of strategies and options, but all of them will result in you buying the securities their company approves.

Doctors are fiduciaries. They tend to your health like a fiduciary financial advisor tends to your wealth. No competent physician would prescribe medicine for you without first doing a thorough examination. A fiduciary will ascertain what your financial goals and objectives are before making any recommendation.

An independent fiduciary may help you determine a conservative approach to building your own personal pension. They will look at your income, expenses, lifestyle changes, and the role taxes play in determining "your number." That number is the amount of money you will need to live comfortably for many years after retirement.

Do you know *your* number?

Next we may help to find choices that make the best "cents" for you and help you better understand the risk and fees involved in your current investments. You may be stunned at the amount of your money being eaten away by high or hidden fees. A broker is not obligated or compelled to verbally share many of those fees with you while a fiduciary is required to do so and to keep you informed of fees you are charged going forward.

Then, we may construct a strategy for estate preservation, protecting your family now and in the years to come. Questions such as the transfer of wealth can be solved with the right attention to your values and goals.

Finally, an independent fiduciary may provide the advice and the tools that will give you genuine peace of mind and confidence with your financial health.

Everyone has a unique family and financial situation, so no answer in this book is going to be perfect for everyone. But, no matter what your choices are going forward, hopefully, this book will provide you with the right questions to ask yourself and your advisors.

CHAPTER 2

Trust and Communication

"Trust is the glue of life. It's the most essential ingredient in effective communication. It's the foundational principle that holds all relationships."
—STEPHEN COVEY

The stock market crash of 2008 and 2009 was a catastrophic series of events that damaged the lives of many millions of people around the globe. That awful time brought more business growth to independent fiduciaries than ever before as consumers became more informed about the shenanigans going on with Wall Street. The giant, secretive firms were exposed, which led to immense distrust as many learned that large firms routinely acted against the interests of their customers.

Because of that awareness, billions of dollars are now flowing out of Wall Street companies with risk-only platforms and ending up with fiduciaries who can offer a combination of strategies for both safety and potential growth — but with emphasis on safety, especially for retirees and those approaching retirement. It is common knowledge that many stockbrokers are transitioning to Registered Investment Advisers every year.

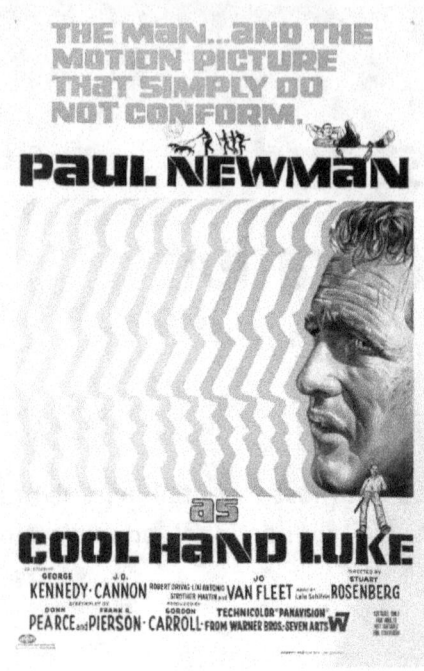

My industry does a lot of surveying. Every single year, without exception, the No. 1 dissatisfaction people seem to have with their advisors is that they don't stay in touch with them on a regular basis. It's the same every year without exception. I can understand why. During the 2008 market crash, stockbrokers were hiding under their desks, avoiding the ringing telephones. Some of their clients had lost half their life's savings in that financial crisis. Anybody can be a hero when business is good. In my opinion, the mark of a true professional is to communicate with the client even if they have bad news to report. In fact, I believe an advisor has an even greater obligation to talk to clients when their portfolios are diminished or in danger.

According to the surveys, advisors remain too aloof to suit their clients, even in the good years. As the warden (Strother Martin) said to Paul Newman in the 1967 classic movie "Cool Hand Luke," "What we've got here is a *failure* to *communicate*."

The Multi-Faceted Approach

The reason why stockbrokers are called stockbrokers is because they broker (sell) stock. A broker is an individual who puts the buyer and the seller together. Think real estate. The real estate broker works both sides of the fence, bringing the buyer and the seller together to make a sale. Stockbrokers are agents who usually represent a large brokerage house. Don't get me wrong. If you are a younger investor and you are in the accumulation phase of your financial life, an experienced stockbroker who has earned your trust can be a tremendous asset. Is accumulation of wealth important to your financial success? You bet it is! But there comes a time when we will, as a matter of priority, begin to be more concerned about keeping what we have accumulated and making wise use of it rather than accumulating more. At some point in the financial timeline, our attention begins to shift to guarding that wealth from plunder, either through imprudent investments or unnecessary taxation. As Robert Kiyosaki, author of "Rich Dad, Poor Dad," says: "In life, it's not how much money you make, it's how much money you keep."

Independent fiduciary advisors, on the other hand, do not work for a firm. They are the firm! They are not brokers who aim to put buyer and seller together; they work for you, the client. That is a critical distinction when your goal is to reduce taxation, plan for the future, establish an income stream throughout retirement, sidestep potential financial threats, create a workable estate plan, and distribute any remaining wealth to heirs as efficiently and smoothly as possible. Let me ask you — how can any of those things be done without good communication? They can't.

> "In life, it's not how much money you make that counts, but how much you keep."
> ~ROBERT KIYOSAKI

I have never really counted the words exchanged between advisor and client during the initial meeting, but I am going to guess and say that I speak one word to the client's 20. There is a reason for that. As my mother used to tell me growing up, "There is a reason why God gave us two ears and one mouth." We don't learn much when we are talking. Listening is the only way to know about the client's hopes, dreams, goals, aspirations, and vision of the future. In the initial meeting, we are getting to know the client and the client is getting to know us. Are we a good fit? Is it mutually beneficial that we work together?

It is during this phase of the advisor/client relationship that we try to determine the client's "why." Money without purpose is merely numbers on paper, or so many digits on a computer screen. When some folks visualize retirement they see themselves traveling to foreign countries, seeing the world. One couple who came into my office a few years ago were very conservative. They had worked hard and saved diligently all of their lives. Their children were well-educated and successful professionals in their own right and needed no help from Mom and Dad. This couple wanted to travel. Paradoxically, they had never been outside the borders of their home state of North Carolina. Not in their entire lives! But for years, the woman had been collecting brochures on Italy, Spain, Greece, and the Holy Land in anticipation of traveling there when they retired. When I asked them to tell me their goals for retirement, she excitedly told me about their plans to see those parts of the world.

Another couple told me that their retirement goals were simple — they just wanted to spoil their five grandchildren.

"They won't be young forever," said the wife. "We want to spend as much time with them as we can while they can still have fun at Carowinds© (a Charlotte-area theme park). We want to enjoy them while they still get a thrill out of going to the movies with Poppa and Meme."

This couple lives on a farm and own horses; they wanted to teach their grandchildren to ride. They told me they could think of no finer thing than to stay at home and spend time with their family.

Let me ask you. Is that necessary information to a financial planner? Absolutely!

When you ask enough questions, you will find that each individual has his or her own vision of what they want money to accomplish. One person may be inclined to leave a substantial legacy for heirs. Another may not. One individual may be passionate about a charity or a church. Another may not. Some people are not legacy-minded at all. One man with whom we worked had expressed the wish to "spend every nickel" of his considerable fortune before he died. He joked that he wanted to "write his last check to the undertaker and have it bounce."

Different strokes for different folks.

Communication Is Key

Nearly all of what a fiduciary advisor does is based on the interchange of communication between advisor and client — from the initial get-acquainted session to the planning sessions that follow when a plan of action is crafted. But the communication must not stop there. At our firm, we like to have, *at a minimum*, quarterly, in-person meetings with our clients to take stock of our progress in meeting their goals. In addition, we send out frequent newsletters via email and the U.S. Postal Service. We host monthly seminars. We host a number of educational events and fun customer appreciation events each year. This open communication is critical to keep refining and adapting our clients' portfolios based upon their needs, which may change over time.

Although I was seldom on the same political side of the fence as former New York City Mayor Ed Koch, back in 1980s, one thing I admired him for was his zeal for public service and his acknowledgment that his performance was always on the line. He was the mayor who was known for constantly asking, "How am I doing?" when he appeared before the public. Financial advisors have a huge responsibility to earn and keep the trust of their clients and should repeatedly ask, "How am I doing?" and not wither from the answer.

Frankly Discuss Risk

In the advisor/client relationship, risk must be discussed and risk tolerance clearly defined.

A few years ago, I was acquainted with a man who had a deathly fear of flying but conquered it. How did he do it? A close relative had died five states away and he wanted to attend the funeral. The only logical thing to do was travel by air. But he literally broke out in cold sweats just thinking about it. Some in his family ridiculed him for the phobia. Because they had no such fear, they branded his feelings as irrational and unfounded, which, of course, they were. But telling him so didn't make him any less afraid. Fortunately for him, he had an uncle who had served in World War II as bombardier in a B-24. The kindly, wise uncle told him of his fear of stepping aboard the plane for the first time, risking his life in combat. He related to him how terrified he was of the noise and the commotion that accompanied the giant plane's takeoff. He shared with his nephew how he shut his eyes and prayed each time the bomber lumbered down the island runway. He told him that he feared the act of flying to a far greater degree than he feared combat. The nephew began to relax and was comforted with the knowledge that someone understood his fear.

Then the uncle made a suggestion. "Why not visit a busy airport terminal and just look at how many planes take off and land safely every day?"

The nephew took him up on it. The uncle had flown several missions without incident in the war. His personal fear of flying gradually subsided. As a businessman after the war, he was also accustomed to flying on commercial airlines. He knew flying was statistically safer than driving. He was also wise enough to know that his nephew's feelings, no matter how irrational, were very real to him. It would do no good to argue or convince him otherwise. Only education would dispel fear. If his nephew saw for himself that hundreds of planes took off and landed each day without incident at the same busy airport, then the odds were pretty good that his flight would also be non-eventful. The point: *Education can dispel fear.*

Here's the other side of that coin. Education can also bring about an awareness of danger. Perhaps you saw the public service advertisement that went viral on the internet last year warning teens of the dangers of texting and driving. The Volkswagen people produced a short film involving a theatre audience waiting to see a movie. They were somehow able to send everyone in the audience a text message to their cellphones in the middle of what appeared at first to be a car commercial. The driver was shown tooling down the road, without a care, scenery rushing by. Then at least a hundred or so cell phones started buzzing and chirping in the audience. A text message was coming in. The camera pans to unsuspecting theatre-goers retrieving their cellphones to read the message. About the time their eyes go to their cellphone screens to read the text, WHAM! The car in the commercial collides with a tree. You can see that it takes a few moments for the stunned movie-goers to understand what just happened. What an effective way to make the point! The film ends with the words, "Cellphone use is now the leading cause of death behind the wheel," superimposed on a broken windshield.

Risk tolerance is a feeling. It cannot be measured with a bar graph or a chart. And feelings are facts, even if they aren't rational. The job of the financial advisor is to educate clients objectively and let them decide for themselves. Once they possess adequate knowledge of the investing landscape they are traversing, they can make a rational risk decision based not on emotion but on fact.

As a financial advisor, I am on the "front lines" of the investing scene. I talk to many investors who do not appreciate the cavalier approach non-fiduciary advisors take to risk. "Don't worry about the market," some tell their clients. "It always averages out to give you a 10 percent gain in the end."

Is that true? We will share some details about that later in the book.

I have a real problem with those who advance the "one-size-fits-all" investing philosophy. What is true for a 40-year-old individual putting kids through school at the peak of his or her career is not true for a 60-year-old on the threshold of retirement. The closer one is to retiring, the more sobering a significant loss of their wealth is to them. Why? Because they are now dealing with nonrenewable resources. During their working years, they can make up losses more easily. Both time and opportunity are on their side. The post-retirement picture is an altogether different story.

As an investor, you simply must be aware of how much risk you are really taking with your portfolio. From where I observe things, the vast majority of investors are unaware of their risk quotient. By that, I mean that they haven't taken into consideration worst-case scenarios. To continue with the flying metaphor, air travel is regarded as quite safe in calm conditions. But when an ice storm is underway, the airlines cancel flights left and right. Why? Because they are aware of the danger. Investing in the stock market can be worth the inherent risk in a predictable market environment but all it takes is a terrorist attack or some other headline halfway around the globe to knock the apparatus to its knees. We have seen that happen, haven't we? That is a major wake-up call to some people, but it shouldn't be if we understand the risks going in and take appropriate measures to deal with them

How often do you discuss risk with your current broker? What would happen to you if another stock market crash took place next year? Are you prepared?

Experience Is a Great Teacher

Sometimes people ask me how I came to start my own firm and what led me to believe so completely in my role as an independent fiduciary. When I got into the investment business, I was initially hired by a Wall Street firm. That's almost all there was more than 30 years ago. (Even today, roughly 85 percent of financial advisors are stockbrokers, and most of those work for the major firms.)

After a couple of years there, I started to question the company's tactics. They were teaching me how to be a salesperson. And, they were dictating to me what I could and could not offer to my clients. Any stockbroker who works for a major firm has one primary role: to sell only what that company approves, albeit limited to the broker-dealer's "Approved List" in *all* cases.

The more I learned about other types of investments that were available, I began to have a deeper understanding of the investment universe as a whole, and it occurred to me that this way of doing business presented a long list of conflicts that weren't in the best interest of the client.

After three years of frustration, I went out on my own, and, in 1983, started my own firm. I nearly starved to death for the next five years! But I survived. They say if you last five years you're going to make it, and I did. At the time, there weren't many mentors in the independent fiduciary business because it was a relatively new approach, so I pretty much had to do everything on my own through trial and error. It was a slow and tough road. But perseverance won out. I am in my mid-50s as I write this book, and have made some giant strides in the past decade.

Independent fiduciary firms can't advertise like the big Wall Street firms. They don't have the budget for massive national advertising campaigns. People immediately recognize logos and brand names from expensive TV commercials or full-page newspaper advertisements. Did you ever wonder how much of the money invested with these firms goes to pay for those expensive ads and their 100-story marble buildings in Manhattan? But, if you can't trust the major firms, why should you trust an independent fiduciary? The best answer I can give is you *shouldn't* trust one until you've built a relationship that allows you to be absolutely certain that trust is warranted.

It takes time. You might trust the name Merrill Lynch®, for example, because you have seen the name on television commercials. But you might have no idea about local, independent, fiduciary financial advisors. You don't see them every day on TV. There's a lot of skepticism in the general public these days. How could there not be with the events surrounding the financial collapse of 2008 and 2009, and the emergence of such brazen hucksters as Bernie Madoff? People have a right to be skeptical.

One of the reasons for writing this book is to explore, in a public forum, areas where trust has been betrayed, and replace the myths and half-truths with the unvarnished truth. To me, whistleblowing is a musical sound — the louder the better — if it alerts unsuspecting investors to the financial traps laid by greedy Wall Street barons and prevents honest consumers from being ensnared.

CHAPTER 3

The Surprising Cost of Hidden Fees

"Never be afraid to raise your voice for honesty and truth and compassion against injustice and lying and greed. If people all over the world … would do this, it would change the earth."
—WILLIAM FAULKNER

When I travel, I don't mind paying extra for comfort and convenience. It costs the hotel money to have thick, high-quality sheets on the bed and fluffy towels in the bathroom. I get that, and I have no problem paying a little extra for comfortable accommodations. What I resent is being tricked and taken advantage of.

For example, one four-star hotel at which I stayed recently offered a room rate of $242 per night on their website. The rate seemed reasonable, so I booked the room online. When I went to check out, the total was $366.20! In all honesty, I would not have minded paying $366 per night. The hotel was clean, the bed was comfortable, there was a nice workout room, an indoor pool, a business center, and an upscale restaurant available to me if I had wished to use them. What little interaction I had with the staff was pleasant. I had no complaints about the service. But what happened to the advertised rate of $242? It was merely a base rate to which the following charges were added:

- Bottled water — $9. You know those "complimentary" bottles of water in the room? I drank one of them and left the other one untouched. They are not free.
- Resort fee — $60. You know those amenities I mentioned? The gym, the pool and the restaurant? The resort fee covered that.
- Garage parking — $25
- Taxes — $30.20
- Grand total = $366.20

See what I mean? It's not so much the money as it is the principle of the thing. The Ponemon Institute© conducted a study in 2006 that concluded sneaky charges and hidden fees cost the average American consumer just shy of $1,000 each year. Larry Ponemon, founder of the research group, revisited the figures in 2009 and estimated that the "sneaky fees" phenomenon has worsened by some 10-20 percent since the study was conducted. [4]

Banks are good at hiding fees. They like to slip in "maintenance fees" and "transaction fees," hoping you won't notice them. Cellphone companies and cable companies are among the chief offenders. Nearly everyone has a cellphone these days, but few of us know how to read our bills. The carriers like to nickel and dime us to death with "service fees," "roaming charges," and "upgrade fees." Researchers estimate that Americans overpay for cellphone service by around $300 per year. And just try to divorce your carrier! You may find out how seriously they take that "pre-nup" you signed (but did not read). There is usually a hefty fee to break off the relationship.

---

[4] Ponemon Institute©. Dec. 8, 2007. "Gotcha Capitalism: How Hidden Fees Rip You Off Every Day – and What You Can Do About It."

Do these companies make their monthly bills hard to read on purpose? We would be naïve to think otherwise. The obfuscation facilitates their mystery charges.

Supermarkets commit pricing subterfuge in a different way. According to a 2011 article in Consumer Reports®, the big corporations that produce our food have for years been shrinking the quantities they put in the packages. It's a backdoor way to raise prices. They do it with everything from breakfast cereal to shaving cream, and hope we don't catch on. The article gave the example of ice cream containers that used to hold 16 ounces, that now hold 14 ounces, and dish-washing detergent that comes in a 24-ounce container now, but used to come in 30 ounces.

I could go on, but you get the idea. Hidden fees are everywhere, *including our investments!*

Transparency in Statements

A 70-year-old widow who came to our office for a free consultation held up a copy of her brokerage statement and said, "I can't make heads or tails of these things." The statement was one of dozens she had brought with her in a small file box. "I used to be an English teacher," she said. "I have several university degrees, but this stuff is gibberish to me. It may as well be in a foreign language!"

I often hear the complaint that brokerage statements are cryptic and almost impossible for the average investor to read. Why is that? Could it be for the same reason the cellphone bills and the cable bills are undecipherable? Do you get the feeling that maybe someone doesn't want us to understand them?

The woman had lost nearly half of her life's savings in the 2008 financial crisis.

"I remember explaining to my broker that I was very conservative," she said.

"And what did your broker say to that?" I asked.

"He told me that he would be conservative in my investments and make sure I was diversified."

A quick survey of her latest statement showed that her advisor had either not followed through on his promise or perhaps did not have the right tools at his disposal to put her in safe investments. Her assets were 90 percent at risk — highly inappropriate for someone of her age.

When we did a line-by-line explanation of her statement for her, we discovered something else that was almost as troubling to her as her losses. Not only had her portfolio lost value, she had paid the brokerage company handsomely every month in mutual fund fees and management fees for the privilege of losing money!

Brokerage Account Fees

It is no big secret that brokerage companies charge commissions. They compete with other brokers by publishing broker commission comparison tables, but the ones I have seen defy comprehension. There are so many asterisks and so much fine print that after a while you are lost. They know the ordinary investor will not try to understand these tables, and that seems to be the point of it all. Imagine going to a restaurant and looking at the menu for the price of a salad. Salad — $4. Then there is one asterisk leading you to a half-inch of fine print at the bottom explaining that there are extra charges for carrot-peeling, tomato slicing, and removing the leaves from the head of lettuce. Another asterisk tacks on a charge for salad dressing and yet another for the waiter's delivery fee. With the added charges, your $4 salad now costs $16 and change.

If you look at a brokerage comparison table from three different brokerage companies, each one is positioning itself as the low-cost commission leader. Broker A, for example, charges only $8 per trade while Broker B charges $15. You conclude that Broker A is cheaper. But if you don't ask questions (the truth often doesn't appear, even in the fine print), you won't know about what it costs to discuss a trade with an agent, or perform some other activity within the account. Some brokers charge such things as "inactivity fees" for leaving the account idle too long. Others charge you just to deposit money into the account.

You don't notice the fees so much if the market is on a roll and your account is making money. But like submerged rocks and sandbars that appear when the tide goes out, market corrections tend to focus attention on these fees.

The average fee you pay a broker to establish an account is between 4-6 percent for a retail mutual fund, or an "A Share" account. Suppose you inherited $100,000 and you take it to a broker.

"How would you like me to invest this?" asks the broker.

"Use your best judgment. Just make money with it," you reply.

So the broker invests the money. A month later, you get your account statement in the mail. It will reflect the broker's commission, which is, let's say, $5,000. Now your balance is $95,000.

As they say on those late-night TV commercials, "But wait! There's more!"

Let's say a portion of the account is invested in mutual funds. Fees for mutual funds range anywhere from 1-3 percent, including turnover costs.

I found the following paragraph interesting. It is taken from the United States Securities and Exchange Commission website under the heading, "Calculating Mutual Fund Fees and Expenses":

> "Fees and expenses are an important consideration in selecting a mutual fund because **these charges lower your returns**. Many investors find it helpful to compare the fees and expenses of different mutual funds before they invest."

And this one:

"A mutual fund's fees and expenses may be more important than you realize. Advertisements, rankings, and ratings often emphasize how well a fund has performed in the past. But studies show that the future is often different. This year's 'No. 1' fund can easily become next year's below-average fund." [5]

More on the real cost of investing in mutual funds later.

Judge Judy™, whose real name is Judith Sheindlin, is the sharp-tongued and sarcastic TV judge who has a reputation for "telling it like it is." I recently came across her book, "Don't Pee on My Leg and Tell Me It's Raining – America's Toughest Family Court Judge Speaks Out." She takes aim at American institutions that insult our intelligence by slipping in unreasonable secret charges and hidden fees, thinking we won't notice. She spares no one, especially financial institutions. I have to say that, even though I seldom catch her courtroom show, I have to agree with her when it comes to hidden fees in the investing world. It is especially bothersome coming from the financial industry because we should be able to trust these people not to blindside us. Fortunately, more and more Americans are catching on. You are too, simply by reading this book.

401(k) Hidden Fees

A law went into effect July 1, 2012, requiring 401(k) plan administrators to give employees full details of all the fees they are paying and I hope they (plan administrators) are complying with the new law. Maybe now plan participants will see just how big of a bite these hidden fees have been taking from their retirement accounts.

---

[5] U.S. Securities and Exchange Commission. Aug. 10, 2010. "Calculating Mutual Fund Fees and Expenses." https://www.sec.gov/investor/tools/mfcc/mfcc-int.htm. Accessed Sept. 22, 2016.

Most American workers don't realize that they are paying any fees at all on their tax-deferred retirement savings plans. AARP conducted a survey and asked a cross-section of employees of large corporations participating in a 401(k) if they thought they were paying fees when they pumped contributions into their plans, and 71 percent said no. Many were shocked to see there were record-keeping fees, administrative fees, and other fees by various names.

Another problem with 401(k)-type plans is that companies allow the third-party managers of these accounts to receive kickbacks (a.k.a. revenue sharing) from the mutual fund companies.

In an eye-opening interview, Ross Kenneth Urken of AOL Daily Finance©, interviewed Robyn Credico, senior consultant at Willis Towers Watson©, a large New York-based human resources consulting firm. In the June 25, 2012, article entitled "401(k) Fees: What You're About to Learn Will Shock You," Credico said, "Sometimes those investment companies say to the record keeper, 'I'll give you a little bit of the investment revenue to offset your record keeping fees.' " [6]

In other words, the big brokerage house or a third-party administrator (TPA) that manages the fund takes an under-the-table cut from your investment and pays off the record keeper. And if your employer isn't paying attention, no one notices that **you** are being cheated. Under the new rules, the U.S. Department of Labor will require 401(k) plan administrators to give employers details of how much they're paying in fees for every $1,000 invested. [7]

In another AOL Daily Finance© article by Adam J. Wiederman entitled, "Hidden 401(k) Fees: The Great Retirement Plan Rip-

---

[6] Ross Kenneth Urkin. AOL.com. June 25, 2012. "401(k) Fees: What You're About to Learn Will Shock You." http://www.aol.com/article/2012/06/25/401k-fees-disclosure-rules-action/20259527/?gen=1. Accessed Sept. 22, 2016.

[7] Ibid.

Off," published Oct. 25, 2012, the writer pulls no punches in exposing the greed of plan administrators.

"The typical 401(k) will steal an average of nearly $155,000 from each worker over a lifetime of saving. The reason for this massive loss of wealth over a lifetime of saving comes down to fees. And those fees are usually expressed in a way that disguises the true cost," the article said.

Wiederman explained that "trading fees are costs incurred when a mutual fund buys or sells an investment, in the form of commissions and bid/ask spreads (the difference between the price the fund actually buys or sells it for versus its market value). And they vary based on how actively a mutual fund is traded." Then he adds, "But good luck trying to figure out how much you're actually paying for trading fees." [8]

Full Disclosure

When people learn the extent to which they are being ripped off by Wall Street, the natural tendency is to wonder what happened to regulation. Isn't the federal government supposed to keep this sort of thing from happening? The truth is, federal regulations allow large stockbrokerage firms to hide fees from their customers, so even a relatively knowledgeable investor is not fully aware of how much of their money is falling through the cracks. Some — but not all — fees associated with a brokerage account can be found in a fund's prospectus, a document that can be hundreds of pages long and written in lengthy, often undecipherable, terminology.

Former U.S. Congressman and Chairman of the Education and Labor Committee George Miller, was one who despised the Wall

---

[8] Adam J. Wiederman. AOL.com. June 5, 2012. "Hidden 401(k) Fees: The Great Retirement Plan Rip-Off." http://www.aol.com/article/2012/06/05/hidden-401k-fees-retirement-plan-ripoff/20251115/?gen=1. Accessed Sept. 22, 2016.

Street crowd's hidden-fee habit. In 2008, he put forth legislation that would force full disclosure to the client of all fees and charges associated with their investments. To use Miller's term, Wall Street attacked the proposal with "ferocity."

In the fall of 2010, the Department of Labor proposed a new rule to make the stockbrokerage industry more accountable. The rule would have required all stockbrokers to become fiduciaries to put their customer's interests above their own. As soon as this rule was proposed, the massive financial industry lobbied very hard against *any and all* restrictions. Their cash had an immense impact as Congress became almost hostile to the Labor Department. After all, they had to protect their biggest donors. Sad to say, little will change as long as the big Wall Street firms have such financial and political power.

The fact that independent fiduciaries are required to disclose all fees in full detail at the beginning of the advisor/client relationship is another compelling reason to seek them. If you have a choice between being bled by hidden fees versus full transparency and disclosure, it's a no-brainer. Fiduciaries cannot accept commissions on securities investments, whereas that is one of the main areas where stockbrokers are compensated. A fiduciary is required to share all the details, while stockbrokers

are not required by law to verbally disclose those commissions to the client.

Mutual Fund Hidden Costs

According to the Wall Street Journal©, the average investor knows how to check the expense ratio of a fund. Yet, in a March 1, 2010, article, "The Hidden Cost of Mutual Funds," market analyst Anna Prior says expense ratios are not the real bottom line. [9]

"There are other costs, not reported in the expense ratio, related to the buying and selling of securities in the portfolio, and those expenses can make a fund two or three times as costly as advertised," writes Prior.

The U.S. Securities and Exchange Commission (SEC) doesn't require stockbrokers to verbally reveal commissions for each transaction they make. Some Wall Street firms even charge for "advertising expenses." Unbelievably, you are paying for the ads to bring them other clients!

So what does an extra percent or two mean to someone who is retiring? Consider the case of one retired couple who love to take annual trips to Maine in their RV. If they are paying fees of 2-3 percent on their portfolio of a million dollars, that's $20,000 to $30,000 a year! It sounds much more onerous when you convert percentages to dollars and cents, doesn't it? If an independent fiduciary advisor can cut those fees in half, it gives the investor an extra $10,000 to $15,000 in traveling money each year. Money that was just falling through the cracks before. Imagine the things they can do with that much extra money besides travel. They can plow the savings back into their investment accounts. They can help with their grandchildren's education. Join the country club they thought they couldn't afford. Your imagination can fill in the

---

[9] Anna Prior. The Wall Street Journal. March 1, 2010. "The Hidden Cost of Mutual Funds."

blanks as to what uses this couple could find for that much extra cash.

If you knew there was $10,000 or $15,000 falling through the cracks in your investment account, when would you want to know about it? A year from now? Ten years from now? How many years have you been with your current stockbroker? That's how many years that money has been disappearing.

Getting to Your Number Quicker

When we are working with pre-retirees on planning their financial future, one question on the minds of many is "what is my number?" How much do I need to have saved up in order to retire comfortably and maintain my current lifestyle? Everyone has a different number.

One of the cleverest commercials that ever aired on this subject was one put out by ING© a few years ago. A guy named Clark is out walking his dog. Under his arm he is carrying a big Styrofoam™ number. You can't see exactly what the number is for his arm, but it is a little over a million. It's "his number." The amount he will need to retire. His neighbor, who is trimming a hedge has a number (well, sort of) sitting on top of the hedge. His number is "Gazillion."

The hedge trimmer asks Clark, "What do you have there?"

"It's my number," says the dog-walker. "The amount I need in order to comfortably retire." Then he asks hedge trimmer if "Gazillion" is his number. The neighbor says, "Yes." Clark the dog-walker shakes his head and asks him how in the world can he plan around a fictitious number like that?!

The neighbor laughs nervously and says he just keeps "throwing money at it and hopes something good will happen."

The point of the ad is obvious. A critical step in retirement planning is determining a specific savings goal and working toward it.

Whatever *your* number is, you will get there a lot sooner if you can avoid paying unnecessary fees along the way. It's like the old expression, "two steps forward, one step back." How much harder will it be to reach your retirement goal if your portfolio is being dinged thousands of dollars each year in fees?

Let's be generous and <u>assume</u> you are getting a 7 percent rate of return each year on your investment portfolio. But, if you have to pay 3 percent in fees to a Wall Street stockbroker, then you only net a 4 percent return. How many more years will you have to work to compensate?

John "Jack" Bogle, founder of The Vanguard Group©, commenting on the impact of investment fees, said "Costs are a crucial part of the equation." In a Frontline/PBS™ documentary that first aired in April 2013, Bogle said, "It doesn't take a genius to know that the bigger the profit of the management company, the smaller the profit investors get. The money managers always want more and that seems natural for most businesses, but it's not right for this business."

Bogle acknowledged that over a 50-year period, even seemingly small fees can compound to take a third or more of your portfolio. It sounds hard to believe, but his numbers are accurate. [10]

"What happens in the fund business is that magic of compound returns is overwhelmed by the tyranny of compounding costs," Bogle said. "It's a mathematical fact. There's no getting around it. But the fact that we don't look at it is too bad for us… If you want to gamble with your retirement money, all I can say is 'be my guest.' But be aware of the mathematical reality… It has been

---

[10] John Bogle, Jason M. Breslow. PBS Frontline. April 23, 2013. "The Train Wreck Awaiting American Retirement."

proven right year after year after year. It can't be proven wrong. It's a mathematical certainty."

Bogle continued, "Do you want to invest in a system where you put up 100 percent of the capital, where you take 100 percent of the risk, and you get 30 percent of the return?"

The outspoken Bogle has quite a following in the investment world. An organization known as Bogleheads® follows the tenets of the Vanguard founder, and its members are quick to point out unreasonable investment expenses and what they consider to be deceptive practices by Wall Street institutions.

Ron Lieber, who writes the "Your Money" column for The New York Times©, echoes the same sentiment.

"The fees may not seem like much," Lieber explained. "You've got $50,000 or $100,000 in your portfolio, and you might lose $500 or $1,000 a year. That's what you would pay to a financial advisor, right? But, if you add that up over 20 or 30 or even 50 years, you're well into six figures as your balance grows. And that's the difference between running out of money before you die, and having a little money left to pass on to your heirs."

CHAPTER 4

How to Ferret out Hidden Fees in Your Accounts

"The foundation stones for a balanced success are honesty, character, integrity, faith, love, and loyalty."
—ZIG ZIGLAR

I saw a clever cartoon strip the other day by J.L. Westover. In the first frame we see a kid holding up a sign that reads, "Free Hugs." In the second frame, a passerby stops and reads the sign. Frame three shows the passerby receiving his free hug. In the fourth frame the hugger says to the passerby, "That will be $20." In the final two frames, the hugger points to a small asterisk at the top of the sign and then flips the sign over to reveal the fine print: *"Consenting to one free hug automatically enrolls you into the triple advantage hugging program which has a $15 monthly fee with an additional activation fee of $20 upon initial enrollment and a $50 cancellation fee."*

Have you noticed an increase in the amount of fine print these days? How many times have you downloaded an application on your smart phone or a program on your computer only to be hit with pages and pages of fine print you have to scroll through and agree to before you can activate the program? Does anyone ever read all that stuff? I certainly don't. I do what most people do. Roll my eyes and click "I agree." Then we wonder why our personal information, including our location at any given time, can be accessed by anyone willing to pay for the data.

The first credit card I remember signing up for in the 1970s came with a paragraph or two of fine print. It was mostly an explanation of the interest rate and how, if I missed a payment, I would be hit by an extra charge, and the interest rate would be even higher. It wasn't all that difficult to read. Nowadays, the credit card companies issue pages and pages of fine print if they merely change the terms of their privacy agreement.

David Cay Johnson, in his book "The Fine Print – How Big Companies Use 'Plain English' To Rob You Blind," takes aim at American corporate giants AT&T®, Bank of America®, and others, accusing them of nickel and diming their customers to death in the fine print of their contracts and making millions of dollars in the process. He makes the point that American consumers have become so accustomed to fine print that we are suspicious of any offer that doesn't come with a copious amount of it. Oddly enough, we have developed a tolerance for the paragraphs and sub-paragraphs of tiny type full of disclaimers and self-serving clauses.

"No other modern country gives corporations the unfettered power found in America to gouge customers, short-change workers, and erect barriers to fair play," writes Johnson.

But paying a few extra dollars more than you should for cable TV pales in comparison to the hundreds of thousands of dollars you could be losing by having your hard-earned retirement savings invested in a format that is robbing you blind.

The Antidote

At Pinehurst Capital, Inc., we enjoy helping investors learn and understand the fees and costs associated with their investments. We use several tools to take a financial snapshot, analyze it, and determine just how much of your money may be falling through the cracks.

The first of these tools is PersonalFund.com© — a subscription service provided by independent investment research and management firm Thomson Reuters Lipper® in Denver, Colorado. PersonalFund.com© researches mutual funds and ferrets out the fees and costs associated with each one. Individuals can sign up for a PersonalFund.com© subscription for $200 per year, or work with an independent fiduciary like Pinehurst Capital, Inc. that includes it free of charge. For most clients, it is an eye-opener to see how much they are *really* paying in costs above and beyond what their stockbroker may have revealed to them. The online service also provides similar, alternatives investments, allowing investors to compare and lower their cost of ownership.

Mutual fund companies are required to publish a prospectus to their shareholders twice a year listing all the fees, expenses and caveats of the fund. Yes, many of the fees and expenses that are exposed by PersonalFund.com© can be found in that document. The only problem is these documents are difficult to read and hard to understand. They are wordy. They consist of pages and pages of legalese and seemingly unintelligible jargon. Far from user-friendly, the very purpose of these documents seems to be to obfuscate rather than inform — which is why most investors roll their eyes and toss the two-pound bundle of paper in the trash can.

The Problem With Loads

Some funds carry "front-end loads." This is a one-time fee charged by the mutual fund company when you invest in the fund. Front-end loads allow stockbrokers to take a big bite out of your money before they actually invest it. These loads can be as high as 8.5 percent! The web-based programs we use point out similar funds without such loads. That way you can compare costs side by side. The computer won't tell you what to do, but it will help you make an educated decision as to whether you should replace the fund you currently own with a less expensive one. (A word of caution here: It can be costly to replace some funds. Look before you leap.)

You could owe a "back-end load" if you sell the current fund. It's all there in the prospectus, which you probably didn't read. And there may be a commission, or front-end load, for buying the replacement fund. What about capital gains taxes? If the fund you are getting rid of is in a taxable account, and it has gone up in value since you got into it, then you may owe capital gains taxes.

Fortunately, the software we use is sophisticated enough to analyze what it will cost you to replace the current fund with a less-expensive alternative fund. It will even report historical returns of each of the funds under consideration.

To put all this in practical terms, let's say you invested $40,000 into a mutual fund and you were charged a 5 percent load. That's $2,000 right off the top you won't have working for you. Now only $38,000 goes into the investment! When you calculate how much that is costing you in compound interest, it's a real punch in the gut.

The Motley Fool©, a media organization that is relentless in exposing Wall Street chicanery, pulls no punches when it comes to loads on mutual funds, calling them "state-of-the-art deception."

Why deception? Because some investors may be led to believe that funds with loads perform better. That is simply not the case, according to The Motley Fool© finance writer Bill Barker, who writes:

"You should be aware that there is no real difference historically between the performance of load funds and no-load funds in terms of year-to-year performance. In fact, according to the latest survey by the mutual fund data analyzer Morningstar®, even excluding the drag on returns if the load were included in the calculation, no-load funds actually have a superior record to load funds over the last 3-year and 5-year periods. Let us repeat that. Funds that impose no cost to purchase have outperformed those that brokers pay themselves to find for their clients."

Barker lets the mutual fund industry have it with both barrels over what he calls "load schemes" and other outright trickery that he says won't show up in the fund's prospectus.

"Because it is so obvious that the arrangement of giving 5 percent of your money away for nothing in return is such a lousy deal, mutual fund companies have begun to realize that people just won't fall for the front-load scheme forever. Something trickier is needed, and thus loads are now not always made explicit to the purchaser. Aside from the front-end load is the ominous-sounding **contingent deferred sales load (CDSL), or back-end load**. This is a real masterpiece of the mutual fund industry. State-of-the-art deception (though we certainly expect to see something else come along at some point). The only purpose of a back-end load appears to be to confuse shareholders and make them think they are buying a no-load fund when they are not. A CDSL is simply a full load in disguise." [11]

---

[11] Bill Barker. The Motley Fool. "Mutual Funds: Costs, Loads." http://www.fool.com/school/mutualfunds/costs/loads.htm. Accessed Sept. 22, 2016.

Morningstar

The reason we use subscription services from Morningstar® is because they are independent. When Morningstar® rates mutual funds, they are 100 percent objective. They base their ratings on mathematical evaluation of past performance. They are quick to let their subscribers know that their research does not constitute buy or sell recommendations. They also rate funds from one to five stars (five being the very best rating) on how well they have performed *after adjusting for risk and accounting for **all sales charges in comparison with similar funds.*** We use Morningstar®'s "fund screener" tool to screen for a particular fund so we can provide an objective analysis for our clients.

Before Morningstar® can issue a rating, they must obtain a great deal of information about the mutual fund company. They take all of that data and all those details and provide that research to subscribers like us. We use it to show investors what they are paying for their existing investments and use the data to find better investment options, if available.

As mentioned in Chapter 3, investors usually look only at the expense ratio to determine what it costs them to own a fund. According to Morningstar®, the average expense ratio for a stock fund in the United States in 2014 was 1.25 percent. That means that the fund must pay 1.25 percent of the money invested in the fund right off the top for various operating expenses. If that is not the "whole story," as Wall Street Journal© (WSJ) writer Anna Prior asserts, then what is the rest of the story? Transaction costs. [12]

Transaction costs can be difficult to find. They are nebulous and don't appear in the prospectus. Mutual fund companies are required to produce a "statement of additional information," but

---

[12] Russell Kinnel, Director of Manager Research. Morningstar. June 2014. "Mutual Fund Expense Ratio Trends."

they do not distribute it to investors as a relevant disclosure. It is available upon request. Fortunately, subscription services such as PersonalFund.com© and Morningstar®, Inc. are good at sniffing out transaction costs if you know where to look.

"One reason trading costs go unreported is their inconsistency, which leaves the fund companies in disagreement about exactly how to calculate those costs," says Prior. "Trying to quantify a fund's trading expenses can be about as easy as performing brain surgery." [13]

But if these costs can make a fund three times more costly than it appears, as Prior claims, we need to examine them and find out exactly what they are.

Transaction Costs

The first one is pretty straightforward. Transactions are made when mutual fund managers buy and sell stocks within the fund. Each time shares are traded, brokerage commissions are generated. According to the WSJ article referenced above, "The Hidden Cost of Mutual Funds," the SEC requires three years of brokerage costs to be disclosed in a fund's "statement of additional information," but the information is usually expressed in dollars, which means you have to do the math to get the full picture of what these trades are costing you. Prior cited Putnam Investments© as an example. In 2009, that fund reported $21.5 million in commissions for its Putnam Voyager fund for the fiscal year ending on July 31, 2009.

"Doing some math, that was equal to 0.69 percent of the fund's $3.12 billion in assets on July 31, on top of a reported expense ratio of 1.26 percent," Prior writes. She adds that commissions typi-

---

[13] Anna Prior. Wall Street Journal. March 1, 2010. "The Hidden Costs of Mutual Funds."

cally make up less than half of a fund's total trading costs. That begs the question, then, where does the rest come from?

Prior lists two other components that are more difficult to identify:

- Bid-ask spreads
- Market impact costs

The bid-ask spread is the difference between the highest price a buyer is willing to pay for a stock and the lowest price at which a seller is willing to sell. How could that end up costing the owner of a mutual fund?

Prior explains:

> "At any given moment, for example, a security may have a bid price of $96 and an asking price of $100. Say a fund bought that security for $100, and the security's value later rises. If the fund decides to sell the security when the asking price is $110 and the spread has stayed the same, the fund will only receive $106. The spread thus cost the seller $4. Over time, spreads can be a significant cost for a fund that does a lot of trading in less-liquid holdings, such as very small stocks."

What are market-impact costs? Prior says these are often the largest component of trading costs – "as much as 1 ½ times brokerage commissions."

A Forbes article on mutual fund costs says this is one of the more difficult costs to calculate: [14]

> "The Bogleheads® define market-impact cost this way: 'A mutual fund making a large transaction in a stock will likely move the stock price before the order is completely filled.' This negatively affects mutual fund owners in three distinct ways. First, individuals receive less favorable prices on certain stocks being

---

[14] Ty A. Bernicke. Forbes. April 4, 2011. "The Real Cost of Owning a Mutual Fund." http://www.forbes.com/2011/04/04/real-cost-mutual-fund-taxes-fees-retirement-bernicke.html. Accessed Sept. 22, 2016.

bought and sold. This occurs when an investor's mutual fund manager is buying or selling large quantities of stock that drives the price artificially higher or lower. Second, a fund manager may alter its investment management strategy to avoid excessive market impact costs. This can happen if a manager chooses to enter and exit stock positions over long time horizons in an effort to mitigate sudden short-term movements in the securities it is trying to sell or acquire. Last, a mutual fund manager may be forced to include less favorable stocks in its portfolios to alleviate the market impact pressure on its favorite stocks. Market impact costs can be a lose-lose situation for mutual fund investors because they may get unfair pricing on both the buy and sell side of stock transactions in addition to having their mutual fund managers compromising their stock-picking prowess to avoid excessive costs."

The bottom line — mutual funds don't figure these costs into their returns. Why? Because every dollar of cost is that much more pressure on the fund to produce gains to offset costs. When investors are blind to the costs, they can't tell where that performance bar needs to be, or if it is being reached. Undisclosed costs cause the fund's performance reporting to be inaccurate. You can't measure the depth of a pond if you can't find the bottom.

High Tech – High Touch

Our goal at Pinehurst Capital, Inc., is to translate the data uncovered by these high-tech programs into information the average investor can understand and use to make informed, competent decisions regarding his or her investments. By their very nature, these computer applications are composed of intricate algorithms. They have to be to confront the various fee structures that characterize mutual funds. As these fees continue to change and expand, our goal is to continue to break down the labyrinth of fees, loads, and transaction costs, and thus de-mystify the investing landscape.

The fact that the methods we use to inform our clients are high-tech makes it that much more imperative that we keep a "high-touch" approach when helping clients. It is the human component that matters most — building and maintaining a relationship built on trust and respect. Each investor is an individual with his or her own financial goals, dreams, desires, and aspirations. Because emotions play such a huge role in making major decisions about money, it is not always about the numbers, but how the individual investor feels about those numbers.

A couple once asked me to meet with them to analyze their current investments. Understandably, they had become friends with their long-time stockbroker. He was like part of the family. The fabric of that relationship had recently become frayed, however, when losses in their portfolio seemed to be like an unpluggable leak. When I showed them the extent of the fees they were paying on their mutual funds and variable annuities, they couldn't believe it. They **wouldn't** believe it. It wasn't possible that their trust could have been so misplaced! Their broker, who was a personable fellow, wasn't really to blame. He was limited on what he was allowed to sell them. Some funds had as many as five different fees and charges — most of them hidden. When I pointed this out to the couple, they were incredulous. They felt betrayed. It was like discovering that a trusted family member had been coming to dinner and stealing their silverware, piece by piece, over the years.

CHAPTER 5

Why Not All
Annuities
Are the Same

We humans like to categorize things quickly and put them in
a box for easy reference. There's a problem with that. In
the process, we tend to create prejudiced stereotypes that
are often far from reality. Hollywood has always been good at
manufacturing stereotypes. How could you tell the good-guy cow-
boys apart from the outlaws? The good guys always wore white
hats. Martians had to be green, and all gangsters wore pinstriped
suits and fedoras.

People often develop strong prejudices in the world of finance,
too. Take annuities for example. Just the mention of the word can
make some people run from the room, or grab a crucifix to ward
off the evil! Why is that? Is it perhaps because they had a bad ex-
perience with an annuity? Or could it be that their Aunt Ethel
heard annuities are terrible from someone in her Thursday night
bridge club? The truth is, most people couldn't pass a 10-question,
true-and-false test about annuities if their lives depended on it.
Most folks don't understand what they are. They base their opinions on what they have heard. Few understand how many varie-

ties of annuities exist and how different they can be, one from another.

Let me put it this way: All coins are currency, but not all currency is coin. All Chevrolets® are cars but not all cars are Chevrolets®. To put an even finer point on it, all sedans are cars, but not all cars are sedans. Within the general category of "automobiles" are endless varieties of vehicles that have endless varieties of features and functions. When we apply that analogy to financial instruments, uninformed consumers tend to slap a once-size-fits-all label on annuities, confusing one type of annuity with another, or judging them all by the characteristics of one or two.

Nutshell History of Annuities

First a little history: The ancient Romans were the first ones to come up with the concept of the annuity. The word itself means "yearly," from the Latin word "annuus," meaning a system of annual payments. Our English words "annual" and "anniversary" are cousin words from the same root.

An annuity is a contract between an insurance company and an individual — a contract that has the capacity of transforming a lump sum of money into an income stream, typically of annual payments. That's why annuities are typically associated with retirement. Fixed payments for life, or for a set period, can make for a secure retirement.

Before Roman soldiers went off into battle, they pooled their money for a variety of reasons. One was to give them a decent burial so their souls wouldn't wander, lost and doomed to an unhappy existence. Another was to provide a yearly stipend for their families back home.

Annuities became commercially viable in England when some bright people began to calculate mortality tables and compile life expectancy figures. The idea next spread to America. In 1719, the

Presbyterian Ministers' Fund was established in Philadelphia, Pennsylvania. At first it was sponsored by the church as a relief fund for widows and children of Presbyterian ministers, but the concept was soon commercialized by insurance companies. [15]

Benjamin Franklin was a fan of annuities. He reportedly left an annuity to the city of Boston in his will that continued to pay out until the early 1990s, and only stopped when the city decided to take a lump-sum payout of the remaining balance. During the Civil War, the Union used annuities to compensate soldiers. President Abraham Lincoln endorsed a plan using annuities to help widows and children of disabled veterans. [16]

When the U.S. stock market collapsed in 1929 and banks were failing at an alarming rate, annuities were safe havens for cash, and became an instant feature of the insurance landscape.

The first variable deferred annuity appeared on the scene in 1952, offered by TIAA-CREF, an insurance organization specializing in supplementing retirement for teachers. In the 1990s, annuities got a major facelift with the introduction of the fixed index annuity in 1995 and riders that made it possible to receive a guaranteed lifetime income without annuitizing the contract. [17] [18]

Kinds of Annuities

Let me begin with this: What do all annuities have in common? They are all issued by insurance companies. They are tax-

---

[15] Cary Majewicz. The Historical Society of Pennsyvania. March 2008. "Collection 3101: Presbyterian Ministers' Fund Records."

[16] Fox Butterfield. The New York Times. April 21, 1990. "From Ben Franklin: A Gift That's Worth Two Fights."

[17] Mark P. Cussen. Investopedia. "Introduction to Annuities." http://www.investopedia.com/university/annuities/. Accessed Sept. 22, 2016.

[18] E.W. Kopf. Casualty Actuarial Society. "The Early History of the Annuity." The Actuary, April/May 2014.

advantaged. Money that grows inside the shell of an annuity is generally tax-deferred — that is, you don't pay taxes on the gains until you make a withdrawal. Beyond that, there are as many variations on the theme as there are flavors at a Baskin Robbins® ice cream shop.

To make things as simple as possible, there are essentially two kinds of annuities:

- Immediate
- Deferred

Immediate annuities begin paying out an income stream immediately. You trade a lump sum of money for guaranteed lifetime income. Once the income stream starts in either the deferred annuity or the immediate annuity, you lose control of the lump sum. You have annuitized the contract and opted for an income stream.

Parking your money in deferred annuities, as their name would suggest, means that you will leave your money invested for a period of time, usually until retirement, and then begin taking withdrawals. In other words, you defer using the account balance for income purposes until later. Meanwhile, you expect the annuity account to accrue gains.

Deferred annuities are typically separated into two different types, which are on opposite ends of the spectrum as far as risk is concerned:

- Fixed
- Variable

Traditional Fixed Annuities

The traditional fixed annuity is considered among the safest investments around. Notice we use the word "traditional" here. That's to set this annuity type apart from all the modified versions that sprang from it, some of which we will discuss later. The traditional fixed annuity is the same basic concept that has been around since the time of Christ. The owner of the contract (annuitant) provides a lump sum in return for a yearly payout, which is guaranteed for a specified period — five years, 10 years, or for one's lifetime. In modern times, these contracts come with a guaranteed interest rate, somewhat like a bank CD, only usually higher and tax-deferred. Most traditional fixed annuity contracts have a minimum guaranteed interest rate — call it a floor — that the rate cannot fall below. Most start the annuity with a lump sum with the option of adding to it over time.

Just as bank CDs have a penalty for early withdrawal, traditional fixed annuities have a surrender period that range typically from three to 10 years. Think of bonds maturing. Once your money has been parked with the insurance company for seven years on an annuity with a seven-year surrender period, there is no surrender charge for full withdrawal. Until then, however, if you withdraw more than the free withdrawal amount per year (usually 10 percent) you will pay a surrender charge on the excess that typically starts at approximately 10 percent and diminishes over the years until the surrender period expires.

Variable Annuities

Variable annuities are stock market investments in an annuity wrapper. Your money is invested in what amounts to mutual funds, only tax-deferred. Can mutual funds lose money? Yes. Are there fees associated with these investments? Yes. And, as we will see, this is where some of the confusion (and bad press) comes into play regarding annuities in general.

Don't get me wrong. Variable annuities are viable investment instruments. They wouldn't exist if they weren't. Are there certain guarantees associated with them? Yes. But there are also risks associated with them that fixed annuities don't have. Here's what the U.S. Securities and Exchange Commission has to say about variable annuities under the heading, "Variable Annuities: What You Should Know":

> "You will pay several charges when you invest in a variable annuity. Be sure you understand all the charges before you invest. **These charges will reduce the value of your account and the return on your investment.**" [19]

The SEC description goes on to list the charges you will likely incur when you invest in a variable annuity.

1. Surrender Charges

Just like fixed annuities, variable annuities have surrender charges for early withdrawal. Variable annuities, like fixed annuities, typically have a provision for "free withdrawals" (not penalized by surrender charges). These are usually around 10 percent, just as in the case of fixed annuities.

2. Mortality and Expense Risk Charges

Here's where the fixed annuities and variable annuities (VAs) part company. "Mortality and expense risk" charges are part and parcel of VAs. What exactly are these fees? The SEC describes them this way:

> "This charge is equal to a certain percentage of your account value, typically in the range of 1.25 percent per year. This charge compensates the insurance company for insurance risks it assumes under the annuity contract. Profit from the mortality-and-expense-risk charge is sometimes used to pay the insurer's costs of selling the variable annuity, such as a commission

---

[19] U.S. Securities and Exchange Commission. "Variable Annuity." http://www.sec.gov/investor/pubs/varannty.htm. Accessed Sept. 22, 2016.

paid to your financial professional for selling the variable annuity to you."[20]

Remember, as with any other investment, the more money you pay in upfront costs and commissions, the slower your investment will grow.

3. Administrative Fees

These are charges for record-keeping and other administrative expenses. This may be charged as a flat account maintenance fee (perhaps $25 or $50 per year) or as a percentage of your account value (typically in the range of 0.15 percent per year).

4. Underlying Fund Expenses

In addition to mutual fund management fees, "underlying fund expenses" translates to you paying the cost of buying and selling securities. In other words, every time a trade is made in the stock market in behalf of your variable annuity account, you are paying for that trade. Where does that money come from? The value of the sub-accounts' mutual funds within your variable annuity contract.

I don't want to sound like a broken record, but remember, *every dollar you pay in fees, loads, and commissions is a dollar that will not be working for you.*

5. Fees and Charges for Insurance Features

A variable annuity is both a security product and an insurance product. One of the biggest reasons stockbrokers like to sell variable annuities to their clients is because they can offer certain features with VAs that an outright market investment might not contain. A variable annuity contract, for example, may contain an

---

[20] Ibid.

option such as a guaranteed death benefit, a provision where, if the sub-accounts lose money, a tacked-on insurance policy would pay the variable annuity owner's heirs the full amount invested. But here's what you need to know. All of those bells and whistles come with additional fees and charges. Make sure you read the prospectus carefully and know what you are paying for each of these features, and ask your stockbroker or insurance professional to help you determine if the coverage is worth the cost.

One point of confusion may be the death benefit. The variable annuity owner may have a rude awakening if the investment portion of his account loses a significant amount of the original principal. The guarantees provided by the insurance company will not benefit the owner of the contract, only his or her heirs. Was the fee associated with that insurance guarantee bundled inside the variable annuity wrapper competitive with the premium on an ordinary life insurance policy? Good question.

Regulation Is a Good Thing

When we go to the supermarket to pick up some beef, we take for granted that the United States Department of Agriculture has thoroughly examined the entire process by which the meat was produced. We are confident that they have inspected the farms where the cattle were raised, the slaughtering process, the refrigerated trucks in which the product was transported to the stores, and the final packaging that takes place in the meat department. That USDA stamp means a lot to us.

Regulation is a good thing in the investment world, too. Fortunately for us consumers, variable annuities are regulated by both the various state departments of insurance (since it is an insurance product) and by the Securities and Exchange Commission (since it is a securities product). All the charges associated with variable annuities are spelled out in the prospectus. The people who sell them are regulated by FINRA, the Financial Industry Regulatory

Authority, Inc. FINRA is not a government agency, but they are a pretty good watchdog to make sure you are told the truth when you buy a financial product. But it is up to you to *read the prospectus* and *ask questions*. My advice? **Ask lots of questions!** And don't buy anything unless you fully understand it. If you ask a question and the answer doesn't seem clear to you, ask it again. And again. Until you are comfortable with the answer.

You don't need any help determining if your right shoe is on your right foot. You know by the feel of it. There is a degree of complexity to annuities, but the individual who is representing them to you should be able to explain them in a way that you fully understand. Only then, after all of your questions are answered to your full satisfaction, should you commit. Never sign anything unless you fully understand what you are agreeing to.

CHAPTER 6

What's All the Fuss Over Fixed Index Annuities?

t was the 1990s. The stock market was on a roll. It was one of the most protracted bull market runs in its history. Pick a stock, any stock — especially one that ended in dot-com — and you could do no wrong. With so much money to be made with such little apparent risk, traditional fixed annuities with their boring fixed interest rates just couldn't compete. Baby boomers, who have always voted with their pocketbooks, were leaving the old-style annuities on the shelves. Pensions were on the wane, and the idea of a lifetime income stream was appealing, but there was a problem. Under the provisions of the traditional fixed annuity, if you wanted to convert your account to an income stream, you had to *annuitize* the contract. This meant giving up control of your principal. Once you annuitized (traded the lump sum for an income stream), there was no going back. For example, let's say a 65-year-old converts a $300,000 traditional fixed annuity to a lifetime income stream with a life-only payout option of $19,000 per year and dies three months later. According to the terms of the contract, the annuitant's heirs would receive nothing. Not the income stream, not the remainder of the principal — nothing! That just didn't sound like a good deal to the new generation of American retirees.

Even in those heady days, when the stock market seemed destined to soar ever upward, there was the nagging realization that 401(k) plans, which were the apparent replacement for pension programs, were not guaranteed. Pensions were a contract, but 401(k)s were dependent on the vagaries of a volatile stock market, as many found out in the 2008 financial crisis.

You could say that the younger generation of investors, who were just starting to think seriously about their retirement as the 20th century came to an end, wanted the best of both worlds. They liked the guarantees offered by fixed annuities. But they couldn't resist the lure of the upside potential of the stock market.

In the early 1990s, insurance companies sensed the wishes of this new crop of investors and decided that it was time to give annuities a major facelift. A lot of forces were at work then. Insurance companies are profit-motivated. It takes a lot of money to build those glass and steel towers that dominate the landscapes of many American cities. They were in competition with Wall Street for the baby boomers' retirement-savings dollars. They saw a need and began taking steps to fill it. In the early 1990s, some of the more forward-thinking insurance companies called in their product-design people and their number-crunchers and put them to work on a solution. What rolled out of those meetings was something called the *fixed index annuity (FIA)*.

Unveiled in 1995, the FIA's main feature was how it produced gains. Instead of using a fixed rate, like the traditional fixed annuity, this new product would track the stock market index, such as the S&P 500, and tabulate the growth at the end of the annuity's contract year, and credit gains to the account accordingly. Insurance companies figured this would appeal to boomers who, when the FIA was introduced, were used to watching the stock market achieve record growth practically every week. The way the FIA worked, when the market went up, so did the balance of your annuity account. When the market went down, you did not participate in those losses. Your gains locked in while you awaited the next upturn. This was called the "ratchet/reset" feature, after the way a ratchet works in a machine. Force exerted in one direction is not exerted in the other.

But there was a trade-off involved with this new product. The product-design folks capped the gains. Otherwise, it could have bankrupted the insurance companies. So, if the market rose 25 percent one year, for example, your gains were capped at, say, 6 percent. Or 4 percent. The insurance company reserved the right to adjust the cap each year depending on the economy and prevailing interest rate.

Why the Name?

The entire purpose of any annuity is to provide income at some point. We will get to changes made in that area in a moment. First, why the name, "fixed index annuity?"

Fixed: The principal is guaranteed.

Index: Returns are tied to a stock market index, such as the S&P 500, the Dow or a combination of several indexes. FIA owners are not *invested* directly in the stock market. Their funds are *linked to* the stock market through the market index the company uses to attribute gains to the account each year.

Annuity: It is a tax-deferred account offered by an insurance company, capable of providing an income stream to its owner. Like all other annuities, FIAs have surrender periods and surrender charges for making withdrawals above the free withdrawal (usually 10 percent per year) amount. With fixed index annuity contracts, surrender charges vary from contract to contract and are usually presented in descending percentages as the surrender period itself expires.

Have you noticed that Americans tend to vote with their pocketbooks for things like cars, homes, clothing, and other staples of life? It is no different with retirement products. According to the Life Insurance and Market Research Association (LIMRA), which tracks annual sales figures of annuity products, indexed annuity sales reached $48.2 billion in 2014 — $9 billion higher than the prior year — a 23 percent increase from 2013. For the first time, indexed annuities held more than a 50 percent market share of all fixed annuity sales in 2014.

LIMRA released the following information on variable annuity sales for 2014:

"Variable annuity (VA) sales fell 4 percent in 2014, totaling $140.1 billion. This represents the lowest annual VA sales since 2009. VA sales were $34.2 billion in the fourth quarter, down 6 percent from the prior year." [21]

A Look Under the Hood

Mechanically savvy car buyers would never consider buying a car without looking under the hood to check out the engine. I can remember when automobile engines were relatively simple and you could perform some minor repairs yourself, if you were so inclined. No longer. What lies under the hood of modern automobiles looks more complex than a rocket engine. Modern cars have computers. There is even talk these days that your automobile could be "hacked." The positive side of that is they are more efficient. OK, so we swapped simplicity with performance, I guess.

When the insurance industry boosted the horsepower of the annuity in the 1990s, they also made it more complex. Take **crediting strategies**, for example. With the old-style traditional fixed

[21] LIMRA. March 12, 2015. "Total U.S. Annuity Sales Improve Three Percent in 2014." http://www.limra.com/Posts/PR/News_Releases/Total_U_S__Annuity_Sales _Improve_Three_Percent_in_2014.aspx. Accessed Sept. 22, 2016.

annuities, what you saw (the declared interest rate) was what you got. Fixed index annuities, however, use the upward movement of a stock market index. But that's not where it ends. The annuity owner has the option of tweaking and fine-tuning the crediting strategies each year on the contract's anniversary date.

The most popular strategy (and the simplest) is the **annual point-to-point**. You take a look at where the index is at the beginning of your contract year and a look at where it is at the end, and calculate the percentage of change. If the ending index value is up, then you receive the difference. If it is down, then zero is your hero. Your contract's value will be protected against market losses.

Most contracts also have a **fixed strategy** for conservative investors. Let's say you just have an itchy feeling that the market is going to have a bad year. You could opt for the fixed strategy (yes, just like the old-style traditional fixed annuity). Or let's say you're just not sure, but you want to hedge your bets. You could split it 50-50 between the annual point-to-point strategy and the fixed strategy. Or 75-25, or in any other percentage combination desired.

Keep in mind, these are all options, giving the owner control over the contract. The owner is not required to change every year. Some owners prefer to "set it and forget it" and are uninterested in tweaking their strategies. We work with a lot of people who are market savvy and like to tinker with the fine adjustments on the crediting strategies available to them. Others, however, prefer to think about their golf swing and leave the finer adjustments to their advisor. Either way is OK with us.

Other Strategies

The *monthly average strategy* is offered on many contracts. The insurance company tracks the monthly index values for one year and, at the end of the year, adds them up and divides by 12. The starting value is subtracted from the monthly average (not the end-of-the-year point). The insurance company takes that figure and divides it by the value of the index at the start of the year. Some find this approach works well when the market is volatile and stock prices fluctuate dramatically.

The *monthly sum strategy* is available in many FIA contracts. You would pick this one if you felt the market would continue in a steady upward trend. With this strategy, as the year progresses, the index value of each month is compared to the month prior. The increases and decreases are added up at the end of the year and, if the final tally is positive, then that is credited to your account. If it is negative, then zero is your hero. At least you didn't lose.

I know I have told you a lot here. It's a bit like asking someone what time it is and they start taking a watch apart and explaining the gears. Why are there so many strategies? They are not meant to confuse you. They are designed to help you and your financial advisor meet your financial goals. Your advisor should have his thumb on the pulse of the market and be able to adjust to the changes in the economy and to market forces. It's a way to get as much out of the market as possible within the confines of the contract without taking on any market risk.

Bonuses

Insurance companies are in competition with brokerage houses, banks, and other insurance companies for our retirement dollars. That's why many of them offer bonuses to attract people to their products. It is not unusual to see bonuses of as much as 10 percent offered to those purchasing a fixed index annuity. That means that if you deposit, say, $200,000, the insurance company adds $20,000 to that working cash and your account is immediately worth $220,000.

It is impossible to describe in great detail all of the provisions, features, and benefits of the FIA here in this format. To get the full picture, work with an independent fiduciary who specializes in retirement income planning. They will be able to explain all of your options until you are out of questions.

Hybrid Annuities

Whenever annuities are discussed for retirement income planning, you will hear the term "hybrid annuity" mentioned. What does that mean? The term "hybrid" means two things combined. When people use the term "hybrid annuity" they are referring to a **fixed index annuity** combined with an **income rider**.

Think of a motorcycle with a sidecar. The annuity itself is the motorcycle, and the income rider is the sidecar. Why does that metaphor fit? Because the motorcycle (in this case, the FIA) can operate independently of the sidecar, but a sidecar (the income rider) goes nowhere without the motorcycle. You can buy a stand-alone FIA, but you can't purchase a stand-alone income rider. The income rider must be attached to the base annuity in order to function. According to LIMRA, in 2014, 69 percent of those purchasing fixed index annuities opted to have the income rider attached. As we go forward I think you will understand why. [22]

Income Riders

Like hybrid cars, hybrid annuities have two engines:
- **Base account**
- **Income account**

Each account functions differently but together they fuel the hybrid annuity. Here's an example:

---

[22] LIMRA. Nov. 18, 2014. "LIMRA Secure Retirement Institute: Total Annuity Sales Fall Two Percent in Third Quarter." http://www.limra.com/Posts/PR/News_Releases/LIMRA_Secure_Retirement_Institute___Total_Annuity_Sales_Fall_Two_Percent_in_Third_Quarter.aspx. Accessed Sept. 22, 2016.

Let's say you deposit $100,000 and the insurance company adds a 10 percent bonus. Both accounts are immediately valued at $110,000. The value of the *base account* now grows based on the stock market index. The value of the *income account* — which is a ledger account and not accessible in a lump sum — grows at a rate fixed and declared in the contract, usually called the "roll-up" rate (more on that later).

The income rider is not the same as the old-style annuitization. With that arrangement, when you opted for a lifetime income, you surrendered control of the account. If you died three months after your payments began, your heirs received nothing. With this newer way, with the hybrid annuity, if you were to pass away shortly after starting your lifetime of payments, your heirs would receive whatever was left in the account as specified by you in the contract. Some riders even have long-term-care provisions that allow two or three times the value of the annuity to be paid out over a period of years if you require long-term care.

Income riders come in various configurations and carry many provisions too numerous to list here. Income riders are known by several names, too:

- **GLWB** – guaranteed lifetime withdrawal benefit
- **GLIB** – guaranteed lifetime income benefit
- **GLIR** – guaranteed lifetime income rider

But all income riders do essentially the same thing — provide a guaranteed pension-like income you can't outlive.

Are income riders free? No, but they don't cost much. Typically 1 percent or less of the annuity balance, annually. Sometimes this cost is expressed outright, or it can be shown as reduced returns. For example, if the annuity earns 6 percent interest one year, and the constant cost of the income rider is 75 bps (basis points), then the net return of the annuity that year would be 5.25 percent.

As we mentioned a few paragraphs earlier, another term you will hear when income riders are discussed is the "**roll-up rate.**" When you tack on the income rider, you are adding what is essentially a "ledger" account that becomes the base from which the income is calculated. The ledger account starts off with the same value as the actual annuity account value and then "rolls up," or accrues interest at a rate set by the insurance carrier. These rates vary from company to company and can be anywhere from 5-8 percent, depending on how your annuity is structured. Typically, once these rates are locked in place, they remain fixed until the income is triggered, or until the end of the roll-up period (usually 10 years). After the roll-up period expires, the annuity owner can extend it for another period at whatever rate is declared at that time.

This "ledger" account is not what we call the "walk-away" money — the amount you would pocket if you just walked away from the contract. That's the FIA's actual account value. When tradespeople talk about annuity products, you will sometimes hear expressions such as, "That's a 10-year walk-away product." That just means that after 10 years there is no surrender charge, and you can take your FIA account balance and any earnings that may have accrued during that time and simply walk away with them, no strings attached. You do not have to annuitize the contract to get your money out of it as with some old-style annuities (probably another reason for the bad rap they sometimes received).

The G stands for Guaranteed

Did you notice that most of the acronyms used for income riders start with a "G?" That stands for guaranteed. How does it work? Are annuities backed by the FDIC like bank certificates of deposit? No. So who guarantees the annuity? The insurance company guarantees all elements of the annuity contract, including the provisions of the income rider. Here are some of the layers of guarantees:

Reinsurance

Insurance companies buy insurance from other insurance companies to provide backup for their contracts.

Legal Reserve System

State departments of insurance require insurance companies to participate in the legal reserve pool before they are allowed to do business in that state. Insurance company failures are rare, but it can happen. With the Legal Reserve System, if an insurance company fails, other insurance companies buy the failed insurance company's book of business and carry out the defunct insurance company's promises.

Reserves

This boils down to the claims-paying capability of the insurance company itself, which is why insurance companies have ratings. Unlike banks, insurance companies are required to sequester a certain portion of their assets (set them aside) for payment of claims. These funds are required by law to be in cash or marketable securities and serve to underwrite the company's claims liability. Neither annuities nor income riders are guaranteed by the FDIC.

Distribution Formulas

To understand how fixed index annuities with income riders work, think of a massive dam. In front of this dam is a river bed. Behind the dam is a large lake. You constructed the dam when you purchased the annuity. The lake behind the dam fills up with the initial deposit and the interest accrued. You regulate the flow of the water from the dam to the riverbed. The longer you allow the dam to collect water, the larger the lake — your eventual income source — grows. At some point, when you turn on the income, the amount you will receive in a steady flow for the rest of your life will be determined by (a) how much you have allowed your income account (the ledger account) to accrue in the way of interest, (b) your age, and (c) a formula worked out by the "engineers" who designed the contract.

If you turn on your income stream and die shortly thereafter, who gets the money represented by the huge lake created by the dam? Your heirs. What if you live to be 110 and the income stream has long since drained the lake dry? Congratulations! You lived a long life and the annuity proved to be costly for the insurance company, but one of the best financial decisions you ever made!

Formulas for the income stream vary from one carrier to another. Typically, if you are between the ages of 60 and 70 years of age, your income may be 5 percent of your "ledger" account per year (paid monthly if you wish). If you start your income between the ages of 70 and 80, you will receive 6 percent of your income base account for life. With most riders, if the accumulation value (actual account value) is higher than the income account value (calculation base), then you are able to use the higher of the two accounts as a calculation base. Once you trigger the income, that amount is locked in for life. Some companies have optional inflation provisions.

Remember, even as detailed as the description offered here is, it is still an overview. I can only cover the basics here. There is not enough space and time to spell out every little nuance of either the FIA or the income rider. But if you cared enough to buy this book, then an open invitation is extended for you to see me personally, or any member of the Pinehurst Capital, Inc. advisory team, and we will provide you with full details in living color. In fact, if you consult any independent fiduciary who specializes in retirement income planning, he or she should be able to fill you in on all the details. These products have proven to be very useful for millions of retirees, but they aren't for everyone. Beware of anyone who tries to "sell" you anything. Also, beware of anyone who claims to be a retirement income counselor and cannot answer simple questions about this unique product.

CHAPTER 7

How Much Risk Are You Taking?

To officially be called a baby boomer, you have to have been born between 1946 and 1964. I was born in 1960, so I qualify. My parents are members of what famous TV news anchorman Tom Brokaw calls "The Greatest Generation" — those who grew up during the Great Depression, saw World War II start and end, and went on to build America to become the richest and most powerful nation on the face of the earth.

As far as my parents, Herman and Mary Perry, are concerned, I have no disagreement with Mr. Brokaw's description. To me they were "The Greatest" generation. So much to be admired. They told me stories of the hard times of the 1930s, when jobs were scarce and money was even scarcer. They knew what it was like to be poor, so they placed a high value on conserving resources and saving money.

Learning to Save

As a financial advisor, I encourage young adults 18 to 25 years old to begin saving for their retirement as soon as possible and to faithfully put at least 15 percent of their wages into a savings program. But it seems that all the good advice in the world will not compel some to plan ahead.

My first "paycheck" job as a teenager was digging ditches for a Fayetteville, North Carolina, construction company. Boy, did I receive a rude awakening at the end of the first week. The paltry amount I thought I would be paid became even smaller after something called "deductions." Income taxes and Social Security taxes. I asked my young boss what FICA stood for. He didn't know. It was just something everybody had taken out of their check. At this rate, I would never be able to buy a car. Fortunately for me, my father gave one to me a short time later — a black 1976 Chevrolet® Monte Carlo with 100,000 miles on it. I drove it until it literally fell apart. But the greatest gift my father gave me was teaching me how to save.

Herman Roger Perry Jr. grew up farming tobacco in rural Wake County, North Carolina, just outside the capital of Raleigh. During the Great Depression, he was a teenager. While people in the cities struggled just to feed themselves, the Perry family always ate well. Food on the farm was plentiful; it was money that was in short supply. So my father learned to save at an early age. When he became an adult, he was careful about spending and dutiful about investing money.

They say deprivation is the soul of appreciation. Because of his experiences, my father was serious about money. When I was 8 years old, he quoted a proverb I never forgot: "A fool and his money are soon parted." It was his favorite answer to my request for anything frivolously expensive. The lesson echoed when I started earning money doing odd jobs around the neighborhood.

"When you earn some money, I want you to give a tenth of it to God at church on Sundays," he told me, "and put four tenths of it into your piggy bank for savings. Then you can spend the rest as you wish."

By the time I was a teenager, I had managed to accumulate a tidy sum of money for a young man, but it was all in the bank earning very little interest. That's when my father gave me my first lesson in investing. He worked for Carolina Power & Light Company, the utility giant that served central North Carolina and has since changed its name. He knew it was a good company, and he ended up working for CP&L for 42 years. He also knew it was a good company in which to invest. CP&L stock paid a handsome yearly dividend. His advice turned out to be right. Although my father never made more than $40,000 per year, he was able to provide four children with a college education and leave my mother comfortable, financially, when he died at age 72.

I had been a financial advisor for seven years when Dad died. It took about three more years before my mother could balance her checkbook. As this book is written, my mother is a pert 90 years old, and I think my father would be pleased to know that she has three times more money now than when my father died 26 years ago.

Playwright George Bernard Shaw said "youth is wasted on the young." I think the old scribe was just jealous. That sentiment is better expressed by a popular saying in France: "If only youth had the knowledge; if only old age had the strength." I was fortunate to have a father who drilled saving into me. It seems to be human nature for most folks to start thinking seriously about the future when they sense that it will one day occur in their case. I say it's usually around 40. That's about the same time you realize you are no longer Superman© or Wonder Woman©, you aren't bulletproof and you can't leap tall buildings in a single bound. It's also about that time of life you realize cholesterol is your Kryptonite.

Financial Phases of Life

There are two phases in a person's financial life: The *accumulation* phase and the *distribution* phase. The accumulation phase is the period from (hopefully) your early 20s until you retire from work. It's when you are earning a paycheck. You use part of that paycheck to pay your bills and (hopefully) you are saving a portion of that paycheck for a retirement goal. That goal starts off as a distant horizon. The older you get, shapes begin to appear on that horizon and you can see your retirement more clearly. But the more years you have on your side, the more risk you can afford to take.

The distribution phase starts at retirement. This is when you sever the umbilical paycheck and begin to tap into what you've saved and invested over the years. My clients who are 65 or older grew up in an era where it was customary to work for one com-

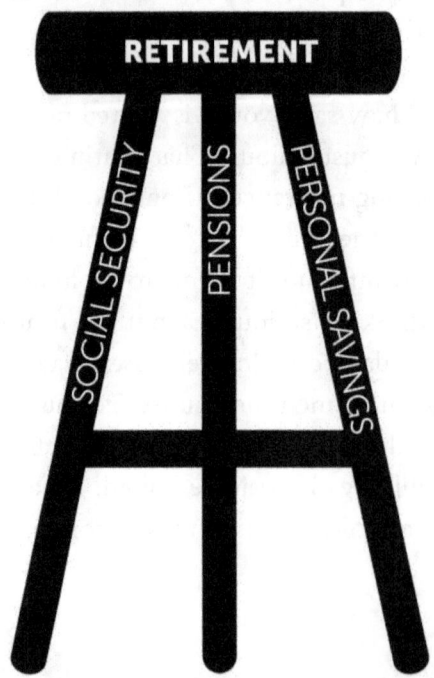

pany for decades and retire with a pension that would provide them with a steady income throughout retirement. Pensions have all but disappeared from the public workplace today.

It used to be that a fitting metaphor for financial support in retirement was a three-legged stool. The tripod consisted of one's Social Security check, pension, and personal savings. With so many without a pension these days, retirees find themselves more and more reliant on their personal savings to supplement Social Security. Some are of the opinion that Social Security is looking a little shaky. If both the pension and Social Security legs go, that leaves you on a pogo stick! But it can get worse. What if your personal savings assets are invested in the stock market, and therefore are at risk? Now you are retired (no more paycheck) and you have to make periodic withdrawals from those equity accounts to pay bills. The risk takes on an even more serious dynamic. Your ace in the hole is that the market always recovers. Historically, that is true. But if you are forced to take money from your investments, particularly in a down market, that money is no longer able to take advantage of a recovery. It is gone forever. When you are in retirement, you simply cannot risk the market taking a serious drop.

What if you hope to retire in three to five years? It is a key fundamental of financial planning to scale back on the risk in your portfolio to make sure nothing catastrophic happens shortly before you retire. What would happen if a market crash like 2008 happened again in the next year or the next several years? Would you still be able to retire? Are you putting all of your funds at risk?

Reverse-Dollar-Cost Averaging

When you are in the accumulation stage of your financial life, you may take advantage of something called dollar-cost averaging. Let's say you have a 401(k) and you contribute the maximum from your paycheck each week to your retirement fund. You work for a generous firm and they match it. Where does that money go? Your employer selects a menu of mutual funds. Participants in the program select from that menu. When the market goes up, the value of your account goes up. Hooray! Right? What happens when the market goes down? Sure, the value of your account goes down a little too, but there is a silver lining in that cloud. Share prices go down! And your regular, steady contribution is buying more shares when the market takes a dip. When the market rebounds, those skinny shares will fatten up and you will be all the richer for it. In short, as long as you are regular with your contributions, dollar-cost averaging will see you through.

By the same token, the very thing that propelled you to prosperity through the accumulation years can have just the opposite effect when you retire *if you don't make some adjustments*. Here's why. You have switched gears. You are now in the distribution phase of your financial life. If you leave your retirement plan invested exactly as it was when you were working, you will now be making regular, steady withdrawals from the account to pay bills. Now you are *selling* shares instead of *buying* them. When the market goes up, the value of your account goes up a little less each time because you are withdrawing money from it. When the market falls, you must now sell more shares to make the same paycheck as before. When the market rebounds, you have less and less in your account to take advantage of the rebound. Your bills will remain the same or increase. Can you see how this process could jeopardize your long-term plans and could result in your running out of money before you run out of time?

One of the myths about the stock market is that it returns "10 percent over the long-term." It's something many brokers are happy to tell you. But, under examination, it's not necessarily true.

In the more than 11 decades since 1900, only four times did the market exceed a 10 percent return in a given decade. That means there were seven decades when the market fell short of that. So, you have a two-out-of-three chance of falling short of your 10 percent goal. [23]

---

[23] Tom DeGrace. Stock Picks System Investment Services. "The Historical Rate of Return for the Stock Market Since 1900." http://www.stockpickssystem.com/historical-rate-of-return/. Accessed Sept. 26, 2016.

Dow Jones Industrial Average **Historical Trends**

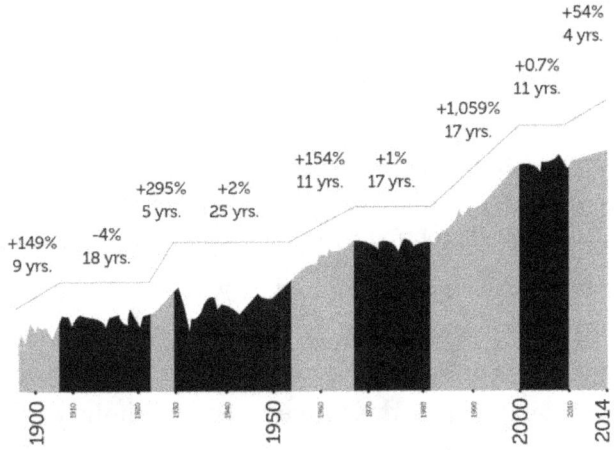

The chart above from Guggenheim Investments© shows eight major periods for the market: four of those eras were bull markets, and four were bear markets. While the market has been trending up in recent years, as this book is written, a chart of the Dow Jones taking a closer look at recent activity shows that a bear market has prevailed.

Dow Jones 2012-2016

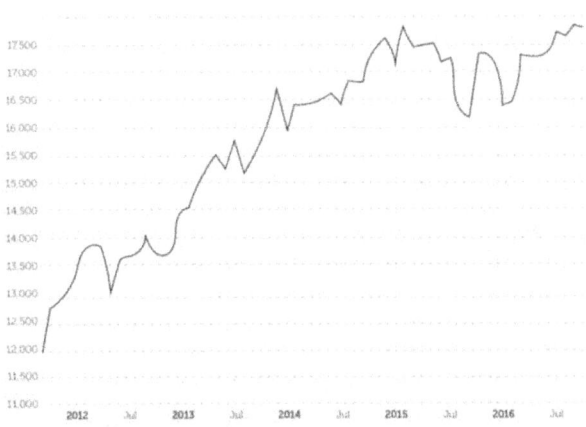

The S&P 500 Index, a leading indicator of the American stock market, hit an all-time high in March 2000. As the so-called "tech bubble" burst, it dropped 46 percent by 2003. Years later, after the index was nearing the previous records in 2007, it dropped again by a huge margin with the 2008 crash. For most, it took until 2012 to rebuild what they had lost beginning in 2000. For Silicon Valley, it took 16 years to return to the same level of employment. [24]

Back in the "good ol' days" of 50 years ago, the volatility of the stock market was somewhat limited. It was acceptable and feasible to leave your retirement savings in the stock market even after you retired. The spikes up and down were not as severe, so one could take money out of their investments without worrying too much about having to sell your shares at a low price if the market dropped.

Because of a more volatile market, a sharp drop can devastate your nest egg and shorten the number of years that your money will last in retirement. Most of my clients 70 years old or older look back fondly on the 1982 to 2000 bull market that made many people a lot of money. The gains were immense, but their fondness for those memories can cloud their view of the years since. The trap is investing in a volatile market the way you did when it was booming.

If you had funds in the stock market in 2000 before the bubble burst, and you have recovered that money, there is still something you can never get back. What is that? *Time!*

If you are retired right now at age 65, can you afford 12 years of recovery if there is a crash? Add in the fact that people are living longer than ever before, and it means you can't afford to take

---

[24] Alistair Charlton. International Business Times. Aug. 18, 2016. "Silicon Valley has taken 16 years to recover from dot-com burst." http://www.ibtimes.co.uk/silicon-valley-has-taken-16-years-recover-dot-com-bubble-burst-1576725. Accessed Sept. 22, 2016.

nearly as much risk after your retirement as you did while you were in the accumulation phase.

Making It a Smooth Transition

The older we get, the less we like change of any kind. So it's ironic that our most significant change financially comes when we are the least amenable to it. That's why it is important to make preparations as early as possible for that eventual day when you stop working and start enjoying retirement.

Some who own their own businesses may find it a challenge to let go. While a competent retirement income planning coach can help you with the financial transition details of such an endeavor, you have to face the psychological ones on your own.

Observation: One of the hardest lessons I try to teach is the gravity of longevity. Many don't seem to have a grasp of how long they are likely to live and how much money they will need to make sure the money lasts as long as they are likely to. This is human nature. No one wants to end up becoming a burden on their children or a ward of the state *and most people don't have to,* if they only do a little planning.

Observation: In recent years, people in my profession are seeing more and more baby boomers enter and approach retirement. Boomers have a more realistic feel for what has happened in the last 15 years than the generation before them. This sensitivity is amplified in the younger boomers. They are much more reluctant to take risks than their older counterparts. Boomers are also more technologically savvy. They do not hesitate to do their own research and find out the real story. For them, the bull and the bear are apt symbols for an unpredictable stock market. Both are dangerous predators whose presence signifies an element of risk.

CHAPTER 8

Lessening Your Risk

So far, we have spent a lot of time detailing the risks your retirement funds must face, as well as the transition that needs to be made in the final years before you retire. By now, you should be asking, "What strategies do you recommend to minimize that risk?" We use a chart called "The Rule of 100." John Bogel, the founder of Vanguard Group©, has long been an innovative thinker in the financial services industry and was the first to create this investment rule. It's investment basics at their elemental best. The simple following chart was first developed by esteemed financial analyst Mike Reese. In the years since, I have modified it considerably, but the theories remain the same.

Bogel's idea was to start with the number 100 and subtract your age. The number you end up with is the maximum amount of your assets you should have at risk — especially if you're going to need those assets to supplement your income in retirement. Risk may be a non-issue for someone with $20 million set aside. They can afford to lose some of it. But for the vast majority of people out there with retirement portfolios, the Rule of 100 is very pertinent indeed.

THE RULE OF 100

100 - CURRENT AGE = (MAXIMUM AMOUNT OF ASSETS AT RISK)

GUARANTEED INVESTMENTS	RISK	RISK-BASED INVESTMENTS

LIQUID CASH RESERVES $_____

GUARANTEED INCOME STREAM _____%

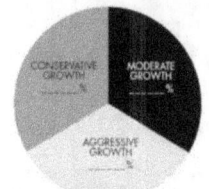

CONSERVATIVE GROWTH ____%

MODERATE GROWTH ____%

AGGRESSIVE GROWTH ____%

- SAFE AND INSURED

- MINIMUM 6 MONTHS' LIVING EXPENSES

- FEES: THE BANK'S SPREAD

- SAFE AND INSURED

- MINIMUM AMOUNT TO SATISFY INCOME NEEDS FOR LIFE, PLUS ALLOWANCE FOR INFLATION

- FEES: 0-1% ANNUALLY

- RISK IS ALL YOURS

- NOT SUITABLE FOR A REGULAR INCOME STREAM

- FEES: 0-5% AND UP ANNUALLY

Essentially, there are two kinds of financial vehicles: Guaranteed and risk-based. In the chart, everything shown to the right of the "risk line" has some element of risk involved. If you are 65 years old, the Rule of 100 means the percentage of risk-based investments should not exceed 35 percent of your total portfolio. Risk-based investments have the potential to make a lot of money. But you can also lose a lot of money. Typical risk-based investments are stocks and mutual funds. You maintain all of the risk while your returns are reduced by charges, fees, and hidden costs. Because of their volatility, these investments are generally not well suited to provide a regular, long-term income stream.

The assets listed to the left of the line are guaranteed and are typically insured by a government agency or private insurance company. There are many types of vehicles available for the left side of the chart, and most are insurance instruments or bank accounts.

The circle on the far left is liquid cash reserves. I recommend that everyone have these reserves on hand, no matter what their age. The cash should be equal to at least six months of living expenses. Some people call it an "emergency fund," or "contingency fund." It's for all those little unwanted surprises life can offer. The car breaks down. The house is damaged by some natural disaster not covered by insurance. Your health, or that of your spouse, suddenly deteriorates. You may need more than six months living expenses. That's just a minimum.

Should you have this reserve money in an account that earns interest? Yes, if you can arrange that. The key is that it be fully liquid. Instantly accessible with a few strokes of a pen or a few pokes of a finger on an ATM machine. Why not use a credit card? Well, you *could* (can you see me wincing at the sound of that?). But the whole idea here is to not derail your retirement savings train. Going into debt is not only stopping that train, it is putting it in reverse!

When it comes to earning interest on your emergency fund, don't expect much. As we write this, bank interest rates are paltry. Under 1 percent. But the keyword is liquid, and the idea is safety. Bank deposits of $250,000 or less are fully insured by the FDIC.

That brings us to the middle circle. Here is a wide array of choices for the investor offering the best of both worlds — good potential rates of return with none of the market risk. Clients may be subject to other types of risk in fixed accounts. Don't look for these from Wall Street stockbrokers. They have little incentive to offer these types of accounts. They (the accounts) do not generate as much in fees as the accounts on the far right of the illustration. You probably won't hear about these accounts unless you are meeting with an independent fiduciary.

The Risk Rut

Many of the investors I speak with on the subject of risk are surprised to hear there are safe alternatives that can allow you to mitigate risk without sacrificing growth potential. Why is that? Because they have been trained by Wall Street to believe that growth and risk go together like a horse and carriage, and you can't have one without the other.

For decades, investors were told by market-based advisors to put faith in a strategy known as "buy-and-hold," or as I like to refer to it, *"buy and hope."* In the stable stock market conditions that existed in the decades of the 1980s and 1990s, buy-and-hold worked well. There was even a period in the 1990s when virtually anything you went with in the stock market was a winner. But with the turn of the 21st century, things began to change, and the stock market became more and more volatile. It became clear to some investors that old investing habits and ideas no longer worked. But it seemed that, for many, the old investing habits were hard to dislodge. They were still in "buy-and-hold" mode, when the investing world had moved on.

The first order of business when I sit down with new clients is to let them talk while I listen. I want to find out where they are. Only then can we determine together where we want to go. This usually begins with what I call a "financial snapshot." They show me their statements and other documents pertaining to their current financial situation. This gives us a "where we are" point from which to start. If it isn't broken, we don't try to fix it. But if their portfolio is not getting them to where they want to be, then we explore options and alternatives.

A typical conversation with new clients sometimes begins like this:

Me: "I see here that you have a large portion of your assets invested in XYZ mutual funds. Why?"

Them: "I don't know. That's what the broker recommended."

Me: "Did you know that it has cost you thousands of dollars?"

Them: "Well, I knew the numbers were off, but they told me just to hang in there, and it would come back."

One couple told me, after losing around 40 percent of their life's savings in the 2008 financial crisis, that the broker used an illustration to try to reassure them that if they were patient they would recoup their losses.

"When the tide goes out, all the boats in the harbor go down with it," their broker told them. "Then, when the tide comes back in, all the boats rise."

This couple has maintained a home on the North Carolina coast for years. They are no stranger to tides. The message in the broker's tidal metaphor was that these things are just part of investing. You win some, and you lose some, but in the end you come out ahead. But what happened to them in 2008 was not business as usual. They were within two years of retirement. They needed that money to maintain their current lifestyle, and now it was gone. This wasn't a case of a normal ebb and flow in market valuation. I couldn't have put it any better than the woman who sat across the table from me:

"This wasn't the tide going out. This was the entire ocean backing three miles away from land!"

Her counter-metaphor was right on target. There was a time when the stock market ebbed and flowed like the tides at the beach, providing a dependable pattern. Those days are gone. If they return, I will write another book to tell you about it, but given the current (as this book is written) manipulation of Wall Street by high-frequency trading and the Federal Reserve, I don't see it happening any time soon. When a market becomes volatile and without a pattern, it is no time to trust a buy-and-hold approach. A properly managed portfolio of stocks, bonds, and alternative investments must be rebalanced periodically.

What About Diversification?

"Don't worry, you are *diversified*," is the mantra of the brokerage houses that would put all the assets of those approaching retirement in investments all correlated to the stock market. But if *all* your assets are tied to the market, whether the Dow, the S&P 500, the NASDAQ, or any other exchange or index that moves with the stock market, you are accepting the full risk that comes with them. Just because your portfolio contains a mixture of at-risk investments (small cap, large cap, bonds, international funds, etc.) does not mean it is diversified. Your investment is still fully at risk to varying degrees. That kind of diversification is a very thin hedge against risk.

Projections Are Not Guarantees

Weather reports are projections, not guarantees. Can you trust a weather projection? Usually. They are made by educated people. And meteorologists don't operate on a profit motive.

It has been some time ago — maybe 15 years — but I remember one January there was a 100 percent chance of snow blanketing the entire state of North Carolina. From the coast to the mountains. That is what the weatherman said, anyway. Every local channel and even the national cable news and weather channels were predicting it. Their weather maps on TV were solid white across the entire state. The weather people on camera excitedly explained that we could expect 8 to 10 inches by morning.

Snow is somewhat of a rarity in North Carolina. Usually only a dusting or two every year. But occasionally, when the conditions are just right, the state can have such a snowfall as the weather folks were describing. When one is predicted, the flatlanders panic and head for the grocery stores, denuding the shelves of bread, milk, water, and other staples. It's a southern phenomenon that forces chuckles of derision out of northerners who take such weather in stride. So that's what happened. Bare shelves. People socked in, prepared for the worst. The next morning — nothing! Not one flake had touched the ground, leaving all the weather people explaining that their predictions are not guarantees. They are doing the best they can with the tools they have.

No one can predict the stock market, either, let alone time its movements so as to capitalize on them. However, that doesn't stop financial analysts from acting like they are gifted with the unique ability to foretell the future. It also doesn't stop some in the financial services industry from promoting the same impression and profiting from it.

One client told me that, when he was in his late 50s, he received an inheritance of $250,000. He knew he needed to invest it, but he didn't know where. He owned a small business that was just taking off, and he said he just didn't have time to do the due diligence himself, nor did he have time to manage the investment. So he took the course of least resistance and checked the yellow pages under "investments" and picked the first advertisement he came across.

It was a large firm I won't name here, but they boast of thousands of offices and "one near you." He entered the glass and steel tower and was greeted by a cheerful receptionist and asked to wait just a few minutes for an available agent. Very professional, he said. A young man greeted them and directed them to a small conference room with a computer terminal and new furniture.

"I was impressed with the surroundings," he said. "I told them I knew very little about investing, but I wanted to put this money I had inherited somewhere where it would grow."

What happened next is typical fare for big brokerage houses. The agent showed him a colorful pie chart on a computer screen. It was all one color until the agent began plugging in numbers. He was told that he should put 35 percent in large-cap growth funds, 25 percent in small-cap growth funds, 20 percent in large-cap value funds, 10 percent in international funds and 10 percent in a money market account so he could write checks if he needed to. The arrangement of his funds in various investments gave the illusion of diversification when, in actuality, 90 percent of his assets were at risk.

What else is wrong with this picture? The client is in his late 50s, which means that in a few years he will be knocking on retirement's door. What if the market tanks just as he makes the transition into withdrawal mode? No problem if he doesn't need that money to supplement his retirement income. Big problem if he does.

Another sleight-of-hand routine is what I call the "big-binder approach." One morning, a couple approaching retirement came to my office for the initial interview and brought with them an elaborate, 130-page binder full of brightly colored bar graphs and pie charts. They had received it from a large brokerage house with which they had invested nearly all their life's savings. The more I studied the material, it was clear that the purpose of the binder was to convince investors of the merits of investing solely in equities. The booklet gave the appearance of accommodating the couple's risk tolerance by giving them three choices:

- **Conservative**
- **Moderate**
- **Aggressive**

The conservative plan projected an 8 percent overall return over time. The moderate plan projected a 10 percent return, and the aggressive plan — for those who were inclined to roll the dice — projected a 12 percent return.

What a bunch of nonsense!

The big binder showed aggressive investors receiving $300,000 for each $100,000 they invested in 2000. Did that happen? Not just no! In reality, those investors would have been lucky to come out with the original $100,000 with which they started. This couple had proof of that with their own account statements, which was why they were talking to me and looking for alternative strategies.

Projections are not guarantees. They call the decade of 2000 to 2010 the "lost decade" because of the volatility of the stock market. There was lots of action, with stocks soaring one week and crashing the next, but when the smoke of that decade had cleared, investors were back where they started. To explain that away, and keep their hypotheticals viable, the big binder people simply produced a chart that goes way back to the previous century to factor in those glory days of the 1980s and 1990s. Smoke and mirrors.

The Recovery Illusion

The statement "the market always recovers" is historically accurate.

I have no problem with the admonition, "Hang in there and you will recover your losses" when it is given to young investors. However, those words can be misleading to those who do not have time to "hang in there."

Some are under the illusion that if they lose 50 percent in a stock market account, they will be back to even when the market regains 50 percent. But think about it. If I have $100,000 in the market and I lose 50 percent, I now have $50,000. If the market goes back up 50 percent, where is my market account now? When I ask that question at my college courses, I will usually see a quick hand in the air and the answer, $100,000. I pause and give the light bulb a chance to go on. Another will offer the correct answer, which is $75,000.

Reducing Risk for Good

Many people just accept financial risk as part of the investing landscape without giving any thought to alternatives that could reduce or even eliminate the risk.

My mother told me the story of a new bride who cooked a ham during the first week of her marriage. The ham was perfect, but the young woman's husband asked her, "Honey, why did you cut off both ends of the ham?"

She didn't know. "It's the way my mother always did it," she explained.

She called her mother to ask why she always cut off both ends of the ham before baking it. Her mother explained that her mother had always done it that way.

Determined to solve the mystery, the young bride called her grandmother.

"Grandma, why did you always slice off the ends of the ham before putting it in the oven?"

"Because my pan was too short, child." Her grandmother replied.

You would be surprised how many people I come across in my line of work who do things the way they have always done them, or copy what others do, never giving any thought that there could be an alternative. Just like the couples mentioned above, only when they are burned by old methods of investing do they look for another possible approach.

So, what exactly are you talking about, Grant?

Well, if you are approaching retirement, why not consider investments that are not correlated with the stock market and place at least a portion of your assets there? Like what?

How about REITs? It stands for real estate investment trust. These are viable investments, yet they aren't market based. Can REITs increase and decrease in value? Yes. Contain risk? Sure. But not **market** risk. As the name implies, a REIT is based on real estate — all kinds of real estate — capable of producing income. Apartment buildings, hospitals, nursing homes, shopping malls, storage facilities, timberlands. How do they generate income?

From rents collected, proceeds of property sales, interest on financing, etc.

Keep in mind, I am neither endorsing nor recommending REITs. They are thought of by some advisors as comparable to dividend-paying growth stocks. They can get hammered if the entire economy suffers, as it did during the 2008 financial crisis. I am merely pointing out that there are alternative investments that are not correlated to the stock market.

How about equipment leasing? Again, I'm not endorsing this, just pointing out that many successful portfolios include equipment-leasing funds, and that they are alternative investments that are not hitched to Wall Street. If you are unfamiliar with the concept, just think of a huge outfit like United Parcel Service® and all those brown trucks that are on the road. Think of huge construction or mining companies and all the heavy equipment they use. What about companies that must maintain square acres of office space in tall buildings? They lease computer equipment and other office hardware. Companies who find it more cost-effective to rent instead of buy will lease anything from gigantic cargo ships to railroad cars.

These investments I've discussed all have their own risks, but please don't miss the point: Risk avoidance means not just lining up for the same Kool-Aid® that Wall Street has been serving up for decades. Talk to a fiduciary and learn what else is out there. There is no one-size-fits-all. No decision should be made before obtaining all the facts. When it comes to putting risk in its place, all it comes down to is getting educated about your options.

CHAPTER 9

Longevity and
Health Concerns

No discussion on risk in retirement would be complete without the mention of longevity. The Society of Actuaries (SOA) zooms in on risks of all kinds. Their 2011 "Risk and Process of Retirement" survey put particular emphasis on longevity. Here's an excerpt from the text of their "Key Findings and Issues" report[25]:

> "The 2011 Risks and Process of Retirement Survey asked respondents about their view of longevity risk. As in 2005, when these questions were last asked, there is more tendency to underestimate rather than overestimate longevity. While some Americans appear to have a moderate grasp of life expectancy in general, many fail to understand the potential consequences of living beyond their planned life expectancy. This study shows many people are not focused on risk management, and making assets last for the rest of their lives is not their highest priority."

---

[25] Society of Actuaries. July 2012. "Key Findings and Issues: Working in Retirement." 2011 Risks and Process of Retirement Survey Report.

They are talking about outliving your resources. Running out of money in your old age and becoming a burden on your family or a ward of the state. It is a real fear on the minds of many Americans. According to a 2010 survey conducted by Allianz Life Insurance Company of North America©, people fear outliving their resources more than they fear death. Here is a quote and a few statistics from their study [26]:

> "Americans fear outliving their money more than they fear death. Life expectancy is increasing and causing people to spend more years in retirement. As pension plans disappear, and Social Security benefits dwindle, many face the challenge of funding their own retirement. The result? Americans are increasingly at risk of outliving their assets."

➤ Between 58 and 60% of the respondents in all age groups worry about longevity.

➤ A surprising 61% of all respondents said they were more scared of outliving their assets than they were of dying. That number climbed to 77% for those aged 44 to 49 and rose even higher (82%) for those in their late 40s who had dependents.

➤ 39% feel they're more likely to be hit by lightning than to get their full due from Social Security. For middle-class respondents, this number rose to 56%.

The Society of Actuaries' interviewers contacted 1,600 people between ages 45 and 80 and found "25 percent of retirees and 21 percent of pre-retirees indicate they have less than $25,000 in savings and investments." Seriously?

---

26   Allianz   Life   Insurance.   2010.   "Reclaiming   the   Future." https://www.allianzlife.com/~/media/files/allianz/documents/ent_991_n.pdf?la=en. Accessed Sept. 22, 2016.

Are you thinking what I'm thinking? As a nation, we are severely unprepared for the future.

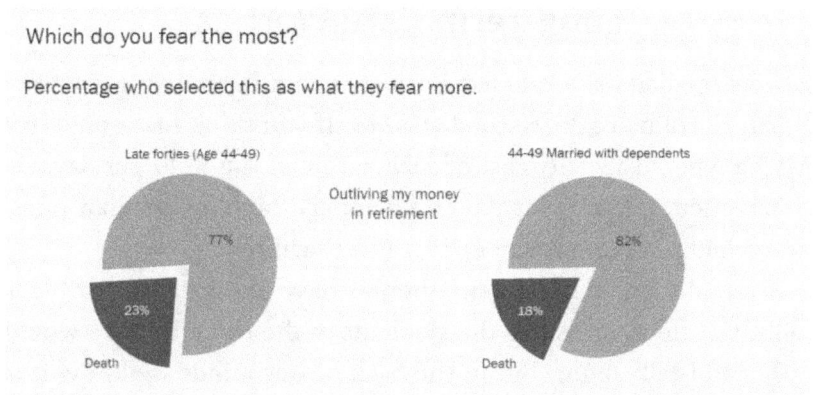

Which do you fear the most?

Percentage who selected this as what they fear more.

The SOA report went on to point out that we are living longer. Life expectancy for men has increased from 66.6 years in 1960 to 75.7 years by 2010. The average life expectancy for women rose from 73.1 years in 1960 to 80.8 years by 2010.

Keep in mind, the way life expectancy is calculated, the longer you have lived, the longer you are likely to live. If you make it to age 65, your chances of living to 90 or beyond are significantly improved. [27]

According to data compiled by the Social Security Administration[28]:

- A man reaching age 65 today can expect to live, on average, until age 86.6.
- A woman turning age 65 today can expect to live, on average, until age 88.8.

---

[27] Society of Actuaries. July 2012. "Key Findings and Issues: Working in Retirement." 2011 Risks and Process of Retirement Survey Report.

[28] Social Security Administration. "Calculators: Life Expectancy." https://www.ssa.gov/planners/lifeexpectancy.html. Accessed Sept. 22, 2016.

- About 1 out of every 4 65-year-olds today will live past age 90, and 1 out of 10 will live past age 95.

Long-Term-Care Worries

The median daily rate for a private room in a nursing home in North Carolina in 2015 stood at $225. If you think that's high, try Alaska where the daily cost of such care will run $711 per day. Or Connecticut — $435 per day. Remember, those are median rates. You could pay more if you opt for nicer facilities. [29]

For baby boomers, nursing homes have always been for older folks, not themselves. It's the elephant in the room that we would rather not talk about. But in the back of our minds we know it is something for which we should plan. Dr. Muriel Gillick, in her 2007 book, "The Denial of Aging," says the following:

> "The latest prediction is that if you are just now turning 65, you have nearly a 50 percent chance of spending some time in a nursing home before you die. Approximately 10 percent of those nursing home stays will be short-term, intended for recuperation after a hospitalization. The remainder will be for the long haul, with discharge to a funeral parlor, not to the family home."

Frank talk, but necessary if we want to control our financial futures.

The LTC Insurance Dilemma

Joe and his wife, Ann, both age 55, are thinking about buying long-term-care insurance. They are shocked to learn that a policy that would pay $225 per day for four years would cost them more than $4,000 per year.

---

[29] Senior Homes. "Nursing Home Cost." http://www.seniorhomes.com/p/nursing-home-cost/. Accessed Sept. 22, 2016.

They also learned the following:

- They would have to be healthy enough to qualify for the policy.
- The premiums could go up in the future.
- They would have to pay extra for inflation protection.
- If they never need the coverage, there is no refund of premium, and no cash value would accrue.

"In other words, this is a little like car insurance," said Joe. "Either use it or lose it."

If Joe and Ann wait until they are age 60 to purchase LTC insurance, it will cost them nearly $5,000 per year. Meanwhile, the cost of long-term care keeps jumping — up 24 percent in a five-year period, according to Genworth Insurance Company's 2013 Cost of Care Survey, based on data from nearly 15,000 long-term-care providers. [30]

Wanda purchased her traditional long-term-care insurance at age 54. She pays $200 per month for the plan. She figured that when she retired she could count on three things to keep her going — a small pension, a few investments, and her Social Security check. But if she were to end up in a nursing home, it could wipe her out financially. She didn't want to become a burden to her children or become a ward of the state. So buying the LTC insurance seemed to be the practical thing to do.

Fifteen years later, at age 67, Wanda receives a letter from her LTC insurance carrier telling her that her $200 monthly premium will almost double to $370. She is faced with a dilemma. She can't afford to drop the policy. She would lose all the money she has paid in. But she can't afford the extra premiums. She can compromise by reducing the benefits. This takes the form of either in-

---

[30] Genworth Financial. March 22, 2013. "Genworth 2013 Cost of Care Survey." 10th ed. https://www.genworth.com/dam/Americas/US/PDFs/Consumer/corporate/cost-of-care/130568_032213.pdf. Accessed Sept. 26, 2016.

creasing what is called the elimination period (the amount of time you must wait before the benefits kick in), or reducing the period of coverage. Both choices amount to increasing the "deductible," and both options are distasteful. As my father used to say, she is "between a rock and a hard place" on this one.

Wanda, Joe, and Ann are not alone. Across America, millions of baby boomers are faced with the same dilemma. You can't afford to have it, and you can't afford not to have it — long-term-care protection, that is.

Even insurance companies that provide traditional LTC coverage are feeling the pinch. An article, entitled "Long-Term Care Dilemma," appeared in the business section of the Chicago Tribune on April 13, 2012, in which Reuters correspondent Kathleen Kingsbury pointed out two factors that are putting the squeeze on carriers — (a) steadily rising costs of long-term care, and (b) an aging population. According to her report, many insurance carriers are leaving the LTC market. She reported that more than 7 million Americans have long-term-care insurance, and premiums on new long-term-care plans are 6-17 percent higher than comparable coverage the previous year. Some providers, she said, are seeking approval for premium increases of as high as 90 percent. [31]

It doesn't take a genius to figure out why many baby boomers are just saying no to traditional long-term-care insurance.

- It's a use-it-or-lose-it proposition.
- The older you get, the higher the premiums.
- Carriers can raise premiums any time.
- Policies are medically underwritten.

---

[31] Kathleen Kingsbury. Reuters, as seen in the Chicago Tribune. April 13, 2012. "Long-term care dilemma." http://articles.chicagotribune.com/2012-04-13/business/sc-cons-0412-save-long-term-care-20120413_1_long-term-care-insurance-individual-policies-home-care. Accessed Sept. 26, 2016.

"Doesn't Medicare Cover That?"

Wait a minute. Isn't some of long-term care covered by Medicare? The short answer is no. Medicare does some wonderful things for senior citizens, but covering long-term care isn't one of them. Here's a quote from the Administration on Aging website, LongTermCare.gov: [32]

> "Medicare **does not pay** the largest part of long-term-care services or personal care — such as help with bathing, or for supervision, often called custodial care. Medicare will help pay for a short stay in a skilled nursing facility, for hospice care, or for home health care if you meet the following conditions:
>
> - You have had a recent, prior hospital stay of **at least 3 days**
>
> - You are admitted to a Medicare-certified nursing facility **within 30 days** of your prior hospital stay
>
> - You **need skilled care**, such as skilled nursing services, physical therapy, or other types of therapy
>
> If you meet all these conditions, Medicare will pay for some of your costs for up to 100 days. For the first 20 days, Medicare pays 100 percent of your costs. For days 21 through 100, you pay your own expenses up to $140.00 per day (as of 2013), and Medicare pays any balance. You pay 100 percent of costs for each day you stay in a skilled nursing facility after day 100."

What About Medicaid?

Medicaid was created to pay for health care for the poor. As things have turned out, however, it has become a benefit for mid-

---

[32] LongTermCare.gov. "Medicare." http://longtermcare.gov/medicare-medicaid-more/medicare/. Accessed Sept. 26, 2016.

dle-class folks who, after having burned through their savings, are forced to rely on the government to pay for their care. I know of many individuals who went from tax-paying, property-owning citizens to wards of the state after their health failed them. As of 2015, Medicaid provides health coverage for 4.6 million senior citizens across America. One reason that number is so high is that some adjust their net worth low enough to qualify for Medicaid, should they become ill. They dispose of their assets (usually by giving them away to their children) to fit into the poverty guidelines, and thereby qualify for Medicaid. Is this illegal? No. Uncle Sam knows it goes on, which is why the government has imposed a five-year look-back period (it used to be three years) to make the practice more difficult.

Medicaid is federally funded, but administered by the state. The rules are strictly enforced. Examiners can audit you at any time to determine if any assets have been transferred out of your name outside the rules. For example, if you give cash or gifts to your grandchildren but were not paid full market value in return, the gifts may be disallowed and not considered viable when calculating your Medicaid eligibility.[33] The reason I point these things out is to show the wisdom to seek the advice of an elder law attorney or competent planning specialist before making such moves.

Some may think that because the IRS allows you to gift $14,000 (as of 2015)[34] to family members that this is outside the scope of the Medicaid audit, but they are mistaken. It counts.

I have found in dealing with the government on these matters that saying, "I didn't know" or "I forgot" doesn't work. It is best to seek the advice of an elder law attorney or a competent planning

[33] Medicaid.gov. "CHIP Eligibility." https://www.medicaid.gov/chip/eligibility-standards/chip-eligibility-standards.html. Accessed Sept. 26, 2016.

[34] IRS. "Frequently Asked Questions on Gift Taxes." https://www.irs.gov/businesses/small-businesses-self-employed/frequently-asked-questions-on-gift-taxes. Accessed Sept. 26, 2016.

specialist when you are in this zone. You may be able to use irrevocable trusts for this type of planning, but it must be structured properly to be effective.

Anyone who has been through this process is acquainted with the term "spend down." If an applicant for Medicaid is close to qualifying for Medicaid but not there yet, he or she must "spend down" assets on the list of allowable (by Medicaid) expenses. On the list are such things as pre-paying funeral expenses and replacing a personal automobile. Anything not on the list will be subject to the "look back."

Qualifying for Medicaid is by no means an optimal solution to the long-term-care dilemma. It puts you at the mercy of the state when it comes to the quality of your long-term care. Facilities that accept Medicaid aren't the finest in the land, and the level of care varies substantially. [35]

Possible New Solutions

When traditional long-term-care insurance first came on the scene in the 1970s, it was affordable for consumers and profitable for insurance companies. As time passed, however, that began to change. Higher health care costs led to higher premiums, which led to fewer enrollees. Insurance carriers began experiencing losses due to a greater number of claims, greater longevity of care recipients and low interest rates. Casualties included such big-name carriers as Prudential Financial© (2012) and MetLife© (2010). Other carriers have been forced to raise premiums in order to stay afloat.

While this was happening, the need for long-term-care coverage became even greater, according to Ed Beeson, writer for the

---

[35] ElderLawAnswers. Aug. 27, 2016. "How to Deal With Medicaid's Five-Year Look-Back Period?" http://www.elderlawanswers.com/how-to-deal-with-medicaids-five-year-look-back-period-12438. Accessed Sept. 26, 2016.

Newark, New Jersey, Star-Ledger©. In a 2012 article, Beeson wrote:

> "Despite the challenges facing the market, experts say the need for long-term care coverage won't go away. The research and consulting firm LIMRA estimates that by 2020 there will be about 12 million Americans who are 65 and older in need of a long-term care policy." [36]

But sometimes when one door closes another one opens. In the early 1990s, insurance companies began to reinvent long-term care.

"Combos"

Hybrid insurance products called "combos" (combination products) by insurance industry insiders have come along in the last few years. Unlike traditional LTC policies, they combine long-term-care coverage with life insurance and annuities. Their big draw is that they provide insureds with more options.

The way the *life insurance combos* work, you can accelerate the death benefit if you become chronically or terminally ill. Insurance carriers have dubbed this a "living benefit" since you don't have to die before the policy pays. There are some caveats to collecting on these policies. Just like traditional long-term care, you must be unable to perform at least two out of six ADLs (activities of daily living), such as eating, dressing, toileting, walking, bathing, and medicating oneself. Gone is the "use-it-or-lose-it" aspect. If the long-term care turns out to be less than the death benefit, your beneficiary gets the rest.

---

[36] Bruce W. Fraser. Financial Planning. June 26, 2014. "New Combo Policies Offer Long-Term Care Option." http://www.financial-planning.com/news/new-combo-policies-offer-long-term-care-option. Accessed Sept. 26, 2016.

Annuity combos come in all varieties, but the general idea is the same as the life insurance product. You may either retire on the money or use it to defray long-term-care costs. Let's say you have a single upfront deposit of $200,000. If you don't need long-term care, then the annuity behaves just like a typical annuity. If you do need care, however, you may be able to use as much as three times your initial premium for long-term care.

These products are still relatively new, but they are becoming more popular with baby boomers who didn't like the idea of paying premiums for something they may never receive. This way, if you "die with your boots on," so to speak, and never need the services of a nursing home or assisted living facility, your money wasn't thrown away. I would offer this word of caution, however. There are many options out there — and options within the options. It pays to seek the help of a professional who knows how the knobs and switches work and can tailor-make these products to suit your needs. That way you get the most value, in the way of benefits, for your premium dollar.

CHAPTER 10

Hope for the Best;
Prepare for the Worst

L ike everyone else over the age of 20, I remember where I was
when the two hijacked passenger jets hit the twin towers of
the World Trade Center on Sept. 11, 2001. I was in my car on
my way to Rocky Mount, North Carolina. I was casually listening
to the radio when the first one hit. They weren't sure what it was
at first.

"Probably a small plane that lost its way in the fog or something," I thought to myself as I parked the car and went inside the
office. I knew something else was wrong, however, as soon as I
turned on the television. There was no fog in New York City that
day. It was a crystal clear morning, just like it was in central North
Carolina. And what had hit the North Tower at 8:46 that morning
was no small plane. Any idea that it was an accident was erased
when another passenger jet hit the South Tower. Later that morning, to my shock and disbelief, two icons of American commerce
lay in smoldering ruins, and the Pentagon had been hit.

The events of what would come to be called "9/11" would have
a ripple effect throughout the world. The New York Stock Exchange closed for a week to prevent an economic collapse. When

the NYSE opened again on Monday, Sept. 17, 2001, The Dow immediately plunged 684 points — the sharpest one-day decline in history up until then. Things grew worse as the week progressed. By the close of business on Friday, the Dow had lost 1,370 points and the S&P Index had lost 11.6 percent. In terms of dollars, experts put the week's losses at $1.4 trillion. [37]

Anything Can Happen, Anytime

Economically speaking, we live in a hair-trigger world. All it takes is one world event to throw even the markets of strong nations into economic chaos. A country half a world away defaults on its debt and within nanoseconds the trading floor on Wall Street reacts. Today, even a rumor can cause a temporary economic crash.

Market watchers call the decade from 2000 to 2010 the "lost decade." The American stock market showed nervous signs of recovery after the events of Sept. 11, 2001, and some thought it was back to business as usual. The 1990s were still fresh in the minds of many investors. "That was only a glitch," they told themselves. How wrong they were! When the financial crisis of 2008 hit, the Dow set another loss record — dropping 777 points in one day. During one week in September 2008, the DJIA fell 14.3 percent or 1,269 points in a single week. This time, it couldn't be blamed on a terrorist attack. Although it appeared to come out of nowhere, the 2008 crash had been brewing for years.

The Housing Bubble

Remember the housing boom between 2001 and 2007? Money was flowing like a river and houses were going up at a dizzying

---

[37] Marc Davis. Sept. 9, 2011. "How September 11 Affected the U.S. Stock Market." http://www.investopedia.com/financial-edge/0911/how-september-11-affected-the-u.s.-stock-market.aspx#ixzz3fF8O0xiW. Accessed Sept. 22, 2016.

rate. It would later become apparent that the nation's lenders were making bad loans. The problem started at the top with the "mega banks" and trickled down to the little guys. In those days, we had what the spin doctors called "creative lending." No job? No problem. Here's a loan for you. Seriously! There was a loan called the "No-Doc NINA," which stood for "No Documentation, No Income, No Assets" necessary. I suppose the assumption was that the property on which the loan was based would stand good for it and that property values would continue to increase. How wrong that assumption would prove to be.

Another exotic mortgage loan of that era was called the "piggyback" loan. This was for folks who wanted to buy a home but couldn't afford the down payment. The solution was simple — do an instant second mortgage. If you couldn't afford the payments, you could take out an adjustable-rate mortgage. The payments would be low to start with and balloon to something unaffordable later.

What was later dubbed the "housing bubble" burst in 2007. Construction stopped virtually overnight across America as property values nosedived. High-rise condominiums built on speculation stood empty, and by 2008 foreclosure signs were popping up in front lawns like dandelions after a spring rain.

News reporters were using expressions such as "mortgage crisis" and "financial crisis" to describe what was happening to the economy. Banks that were considered "too big to fail" were falling like dominos — Bear Stearns, Lehman Brothers, Goldman Sachs, and Morgan Stanley©. The American people began to realize that these lords of finance were perched atop mountains of bad debt they had been accumulating for years.

"We just got numb to the whole thing after a while," said one of my clients. "Every morning when we turned on the television we expected another bailout. Nothing surprised us anymore."

The bail-out list would eventually include such venerable institutions as Merrill Lynch®, Fannie Mae™, Freddie Mac™, WaMu (Washington Mutual), Citigroup©, and AIG© (American International Group).

From Wall Street to Main Street

As a financial advisor, I felt like a first responder to a disaster during the financial crisis of 2008. I saw firsthand the personal toll it exacted. Looking back, I am happy that my long-time clients who had followed the safe-money investing strategies we advocated had weathered the financial storm with few losses. This was primarily through the use of stress-tested, low-risk portfolios. But when I conducted my educational workshops, I heard the horror stories of those who did not fare as well. At one such workshop in the fall of 2008, I noticed that the mood in the small auditorium in which I was to speak seemed somber, and I thought I knew why. It had just hit the news that Lehman Brothers, one of the big-boy banks on Wall Street that was considered "too big to fail," had just declared bankruptcy. The Dow Jones had lost almost 1,000 points in one week. The Federal Reserve was going to bail out American International Group with an $85 billion loan.

I had planned to talk about estate planning, but I knew that these people were stunned by what was happening on Wall Street, so I just turned off my PowerPoint projector and opened up the meeting to questions. There were plenty of them.

"Why didn't our financial advisor warn us this was coming?"

"What should we do now? Stay in the market? Move to cash?"

"We were going to retire next year. Now what?"

"When do you think the market will recover?"

Obviously, I had no satisfying answers for some of those questions. If I could have seen into the future and predicted that many of these good people would lose as much as half their life's savings in the market crash of 2008, I would have started taking out full-page ads in USA Today® to warn them. But I had no crystal ball. No one saw it coming.

Little could be done to replace what was lost. The solution for many of those folks would be postponing retirement and working for years past their original target date. Some would have to put their dreams aside and pare down their expenses just to get by. I could not blame those people for feeling betrayed.

"Our broker just won't return our calls," blurted one woman.

"My broker told me to just 'hang in there and it will bounce back'," said one man in a tone of frustration. I explained to him that his broker was right, in a way. Markets do eventually rebound, but sometimes it takes decades.

"Decades I don't have," he said, to which I could only nod in agreement.

One couple with whom I met privately later that week told me another sad story. Before the crash, they had a retirement nest egg of just over $700,000. At the advice of their broker, they had invested it in a mixture of bonds, stocks, mutual funds, and variable annuities. They checked their statement online just before coming in for their appointment, and they were down to approximately $420,000. They owned a small but thriving nursery and landscaping business. Their plans were to turn the business over to their son and his wife. They figured that if they were careful, between their savings and their Social Security they could live comfortably and even do some of the traveling they had always dreamed of. Now, those dreams were shattered, and they had to face the harsh reality of working at least another four years or so.

A Plug for HiddenLevers©

It is impossible to predict what will happen next in this topsy-turvy world. But just because we can't foresee the future doesn't mean we don't prepare for it. In Chapter 4 of this book, I mentioned some of the modern technology we have embraced at Pinehurst Capital, Inc. to ferret out hidden fees and unnecessary investing charges. Another powerful tool we use is from a company called HiddenLevers©. Founded in 2010, HiddenLevers© makes software that allows investors to see what could likely happen to their portfolios, and to the economy, should certain events take place in the world.

What would happen, for instance, if you woke up one morning, turned on CNN® News only to learn that China's economy was in a panic and the Chinese stock market was in a free fall? HiddenLevers© software can analyze what impact that would have on your entire investment portfolio.

What if another oil embargo causes fuel prices to skyrocket overnight, sending ripple effects throughout the world economy? What if computer hackers manage to disable Wall Street? There are dozens of "what if" scenarios. HiddenLevers© analyzes millions of data points and 100 economic indicators to give your portfolio a "stress test" to see how your portfolio would be affected. Not only does it offer this prediction, but it offers risk-management strategies to offset such possible losses.

The program was developed by Massachusetts Institute of Technology computer science maven Praveen Ghanta, along with Raj Udeshi, whose background is in finance. Barrons® magazine, in an Aug. 27, 2011, article entitled, "How to Get Ready for the Next Big Crisis," calls the technology a "black swan in a box." "Black swan" is Wall Street jargon for any unexpected major economic event that dramatically affects markets. [38]

---

[38] Lauren Foster. Barrons. Aug. 27, 2011. "How to Get Ready for the Next Big Crisis." http://www.barrons.com/articles/SB50001424052702303599904576526841302376056. Accessed Sept. 22, 2016.

In turn, they can take those results and help clarify what kind of investments may be right for you in case of future major events. We often use it to compare different investment strategies to see what approach an investor can take to minimize the risks.

Anyone who has ever been lost on a road trip will understand what I am about to say next: "Thank God for global positioning systems." Instead of finding the nearest gas station to buy a map or ask a local for directions, all you have to do is enter your destination in your phone and let it talk you there. It will even draw you a map!

Investing in a volatile and unpredictable market is fraught with pitfalls and detours. Why not take advantage of the latest technology that will help us avoid these dangers? Naturally, the technology is patented and rather costly for the individual investor. But a financial advisory firm should be able to afford the monthly subscription fees. Programs like HiddenLevers© and others that identify where risk exposure lies are a necessity in today's investing environment. Keep in mind, the software doesn't give you the protection; it helps you identify strategies to minimize risk exposure.

CHAPTER 11

Planning
vs.
Procrastination

There is a timeless proverb that says: "knowledge is power," and I halfway agree with it. What I mean is, knowledge is only power if you apply it.

In one of my college courses, the professor gave us a lesson on the difference between knowledge, wisdom, and understanding.

"Knowledge is having the facts," he said. "For example, suppose that you are standing in the middle of the road with a tractor-trailer rig heading your direction at a high rate of speed. Your mind is in possession of several facts. The truck is made of hard metal. You are made of soft tissue. The truck is moving fast. You are in its way."

"Understanding is having a grasp of relationships and consequences," he continued. "You grasp the consequences of remaining in the middle of the road. You perceive the danger in which you find yourself."

"Wisdom," he concluded, "is getting off the road."

The investing world has changed dramatically in the last few decades, but, believe it or not, there are some out there who insist on using strategies and methods from days gone by. Then they are puzzled when their portfolios lose ground, and their retirement goals are pushed further back.

The 4 Percent Rule

Take the "4 percent withdrawal rule" for example. For years, brokerage firms and financial advisors tied to the stock market have promoted the idea of the 4 percent withdrawal "rule" as if it were the holy grail of retirement income planning. To make the math easy, say you have $1 million in a brokerage account. The 4 percent withdrawal rule says that you should be able to withdraw 4 percent from the account per year ($40,000), and even add slightly to that figure each year for inflation, and never run out of money in retirement. The concept hinged on rebalancing the account each year to just the right mixture of stocks and bonds. Notice I use the past tense here. That's because the concept doesn't work anymore unless you are among the wealthiest.

The 4 percent withdrawal rule was the brainchild of three professors at Trinity University in San Antonio, Texas in the mid-1990s. Their calculations and projections were based on stock market data available at the time — the 1990s — one of the longest bull markets in recent memory. So what happened? The 1990s ended with the bursting of the tech bubble in 2000 and a sideways market for the next decade. Even though the 4 percent withdrawal rule no longer worked, some advisors who were die-hard proponents still promoted it.

Other factors that make the 4 percent rule invalid are:
- Most Americans are not super wealthy.
- People are living longer these days.
- The stock market became more volatile in the 21st century.

In an article entitled "Forget the 4% Withdrawal Rule," published by Money® magazine in 2014, Wade Pfau, professor of retirement income at The American College, lowers the 4 percent withdrawal projection down to 2.22 percent. That means that if you can bring $1 million to the retirement table, and you want it to last the rest of your life, you have to ratchet your annual withdrawal down to a little over $20,000 per year — which is fine if you are comfortable living on the border of the national poverty line.

Here are some other headlines that read like obituaries for the "4 Percent Rule."

- **The 4 Percent Rule No Longer Applies For Most Retirees** ~ CNBC®, Kelley Holland, April 22, 2015. "Part of the problem with the 4 percent rule is that it was developed in the 1990s when interest rates were significantly higher."
- **4% Rule for Retirement Withdrawals Is Golden No More** ~ New York Times®, 2013. "Many financial advisers are rejecting the 4 percent rule as out of touch with present realities."
- **How Much to Withdraw from Retirement Savings** ~ Forbes Magazine® 2013: "When the 4% rule emerged, investment portfolios were earning about 8% annually. Today, they're generally in the 3 to 4% range."
- **Retirees May Need to Rethink 4% Rule** ~ AARP 2013 "… new research by Morningstar Investment Management® suggests that relying on that 4 percent rule of thumb today is risky, thanks to a market in which bond yields and dividends have hovered at record lows for years."

Would you believe that, still, in the face of all the evidence to the contrary, some financial advisors still preach the 4 percent rule as if it were gospel? Maybe they just haven't been reading the headlines. Let's hope it is ignorance and not purposeful misdirection for the sake of greed. It could be that this investing approach is the only one they know. Whatever the case, they need to get in step with the times.

Why People Procrastinate

Some animals will stop in their tracks and stand there motionless when you shine a light in their eyes. In North Carolina, where I live, it is illegal to hunt animals with a spotlight because some of them — deer in particular — freeze when a bright light is pointed at them. I suppose that's where we get the expression "like a deer in the headlights" to describe the way some people fail to take action to escape danger.

Some folks react that way to making decisions regarding their finances. Faced with too many important decisions and conflicting expert opinions in the media, they take the course of least resistance and simply do nothing. Here are some other reasons people put off planning for retirement:

• **"I'm too busy."** I hear this one from the younger crowd, still in their accumulation years. Perhaps they are raising families and building their careers. I'm sure they have full lives. To them, retirement is a "someday" thing, far off on the distant horizon. Take it from a baby boomer. It won't be long before the sand in your hourglass becomes bottom-heavy. Every year that goes by unattended is a year that is lost forever. Why not take advantage of the free consultation that most fiduciary planners offer. It's just a get-acquainted conversation to explore your options.

• **"I don't have enough money to worry about."** Where do you start anything? At the beginning, right? You may not be able to produce a comprehensive plan with all the answers. But if you have no money and lots of debt, that tells me you need to start planning right away. That's the only way to get a base from which you can operate. To start small is better than not starting at all!

• **"It's too soon to start."** Some have the notion that they can't start planning for retirement until they are almost ready to retire. Remember, money has a time value. The more time you have on your side, the easier your path to retirement will be.

- **"It's too late to start."** It's never too late to start. There is a constant flow of new products and new strategies in the field of retirement planning. If you have already retired, you may be pleasantly surprised when you sit down with a fiduciary and explore what options are open to you.

- **"I can handle it myself."** Some folks who are computer savvy and handy with numbers would rather go it alone. I understand this. I admire the do-it-yourself spirit. But just as you wouldn't take that approach with your health, you shouldn't take that approach with your wealth. The idea of self-dentistry or self-surgery is laughable, isn't it? But losing thousands of dollars in your portfolio isn't so funny. Neither is paying thousands of dollars in unnecessary taxes. At least have a conversation with a professional fiduciary. There may be options out there that you know nothing about. It may prove worth your time to at least look into them.

Those are just a few of the reasons for procrastination that I can think of.

I attended a continuing education seminar once, and the speaker gave the audience an excellent lesson on procrastination. He handed each of us a wooden disc with the word "TUIT" printed on each side. As he strolled up the center aisle, distributing the wooden discs, he talked about a personal friend who postponed seeing a doctor until it was too late for medical help. As most people know, when you turn 50 you should have a colonoscopy and a follow-up at least every five years. Well, his friend had postponed getting this little check-up because he had what the speaker called "doctorphobia." When he was in his late 60s, he died unnecessarily of colon cancer.

"You are probably wondering what this story has to do with the wooden disc I have given you," the speaker said. "Hold it in your hand and read what is inscribed on either side. What I have given you is a TUIT. Notice the shape of the TUIT. It is a round

TUIT. If you have been putting off something you know you should do until you get **around to it**, now you have **a round TU-IT — so do it!**

Thank you, dear reader, for coming with me this far. I hope you have benefitted by what we have discussed thus far in this book, and I commend you for your desire to broaden your base of knowledge. If you come away with an enhanced understanding of investing, wealth preservation, and distribution, then I have accomplished most of what I set out to do.

My mission is to empower you as an investor and saver to avoid getting trapped by layers of hidden charges levied upon the American investing public. When you purchase a car, a home, or even an article of clothing — anything that comes with a stated price — what you pay is straightforward. In today's investment world, many of these fees and charges are not disclosed. Those that are disclosed are in fine print so you must know where to look to find them.

As I said at the beginning of this book, knowing this threat to your financial security exists is power — but only if you take action to prevent it from happening to you.

About the Author

H. Grant Perry, ChFC™, is Founding Principal of Pinehurst Capital, Inc. He is an experienced advisor who focuses on retirement income solutions, IRAs and 401(k) plans. Grant is widely recognized for his knowledge of undisclosed fees and false performance reporting by mutual fund companies and other financial institutions. He has trademarks on three proprietary methods of identifying phantom taxes, hidden fees, and phony performance claims, and makes these available to all scheduled appointments at no cost.

In 1978, North Carolina Senator Jesse Helms awarded Grant an appointment to the United States Military Academy at West Point; but Grant opted for a career in finance and completed five years of advanced studies at The American College. Grant is a popular and prominent public speaker and columnist. He has lectured at Methodist University's Center for Entrepreneurship, was the original financial columnist for Up & Coming Magazine© and is a contributing writer for Carolina Business Journal®. He is an Elder at Community Presbyterian Church in Pinehurst, North Carolina, serves on the endowment committee, and is chairman of the finance ministry. Pinehurst Capital, Inc., Grant's Registered Investment Advisory practice, is a strong supporter of The Patriot

Foundation©, a Fort Bragg, North Carolina, charity with the mission of providing support for the families of the base's airborne and Special Operations soldiers and other selected warriors. Grant is an avid sportsman and is the founder of the Sandhills Sporting Society, a charitable organization of golfers, hunters, and fishing lovers. He was born and raised in Spring Lake, North Carolina, and now lives and works in Pinehurst, North Carolina.